Literature
and Evil

By the same author

Story of the Eye (novel)
Blue of Noon (novel)
L'Abbé C (novel)
My Mother, Madame Edwarda, The Dead Man (novels)
Eroticism (philosophy)

Literature and Evil

Essays by
Georges Bataille

Translated by
Alastair Hamilton

If only he had been alive to make sense of you,

Happy Birthday. 1993.

Love Daniel.

Marion Boyars
London · New York

Republished in Great Britain and the United States in 1985
by Marion Boyars Publishers
24 Lacy Road, London SW15 1NL
237 East 39th Street, New York, NY 10016

Reprinted in 1990, 1993

Originally published in France in 1957
as *La Littérature et le Mal* by Editions Gallimard, Paris

© Editions Gallimard 1957
© This translation Marion Boyars Ltd, 1973, 1985, 1990, 1993

British Library Cataloguing in Publication Data
Bataille, Georges
   Literature and evil.
   1. Evil in literature. 2. Literature, Modern —
   History and criticism
I. Title II. La littérature et le mal. *English*
   809'.933' PN710

Library of Congress Cataloging in Publication Data
Bataille, Georges, 1897–1962.
   Literature and evil.
   Translation of: La Littérature et le mal.
   Reprint. Originally published: London: Calder and
Boyars, 1973 (Signature series)
   1. Evil in literature. 2. Literature, Modern —
History and criticism. I. Title.
PN56.E75B3 13   1983   809'.9338 83–25872

ISBN 0–7145–0346–0 paperback
       0–7145–0345–2 cloth

Typeset by Photosetting, Yeovil, Somerset
Printed by Itchen Printers, Southampton

CONTENTS

PREFACE

I belong to a turbulent generation, born to literary life in the tumult of surrealism. In the years after the Great War there was a feeling which was about to overflow. Literature was stifling within its limitations and seemed pregnant with revolution.

These studies, which are so strikingly coherent, were written by a mature man. Yet they were generated in the turbulence of his youth, and they faintly echo this.

I find it significant that a part of the first version of these essays should have appeared in *Critique*, a review which owed its success to its serious character. But I must add that, if I occasionally had to rewrite them, it is because, at first, I could provide no more than an obscure expression of my ideas owing to the turmoil in my mind. Turmoil is fundamental to my entire study; it is the very essence of my book. But the time has come to strive towards a clarity of consciousness. I say the time has come... But there are moments when time almost seems to be lacking, or at any rate pressing.

These studies are the result of my attempts to extract the essence of literature. Literature is either the essential or nothing. I believe that the Evil – an acute form of Evil – which it expresses, has a sovereign value for us. But this concept does not exclude morality: on the contrary, it demands a 'hypermorality'.

Literature is *communication*. Communication requires loyalty. A rigorous morality results from complicity in the knowledge of Evil, which is the basis of intense communication.

Literature is not innocent. It is guilty and should admit itself so. Action alone has its rights, its prerogatives. I wanted to prove that literature is a return to childhood. But has the childhood that governs it a truth of its own? Before the necessity of *action*, we are overwhelmed by Kafka's honesty, which abrogates no rights for itself. Whatever the lesson contained in Genet's books, Sartre's defence is inadmissible. Literature *had* to plead guilty.[1]

NOTES

1. I have omitted from this collection a study on *Les Chants de Maldoror* which stood so well on its own that it seemed superfluous. There is hardly any point in my saying that Lautreamont's poetry corresponds to my theories. Are his poems not literature pleading guilty? They baffle us, but if they can be understood it is surely in the light of my interpretation.

EMILY BRONTË

Emily Brontë, of all women, seems to have been the object of a privileged curse. Her short life was only moderately unhappy. Yet, keeping her moral purity intact, she had a profound experience of the abyss of Evil. Though few people could have been more severe, more courageous or more proper, she fathomed the very depths of Evil.

This was the task of literature, imagination and dream. Her life, over by the time she was thirty, was completely sheltered. She was born in 1818 and rarely left the Yorkshire vicarage set in a rugged wasteland where her father, an Irish pastor, gave her an austere education, but little else. Her mother died early and her two sisters were extremely strict. A dissipated brother ruined himself somewhat romantically. We know that in the austerity of the vicarage, the three Brontë sisters lived in a frenzy of literary creativity. They were bound together by a day to day intimacy, though Emily nevertheless continued to preserve that moral solitude in which the phantoms of her imagination developed. Reserved as she was, she appears to have been good, active and devoted, indeed gentleness itself. She lived in a sort of silence which, it seemed, only literature could disrupt. The morning she died, after a brief lung disease, she got up at the usual time, joined her family without uttering a word and expired before midday, without even going back to bed. She had not wanted to see a doctor.

She left behind her a short collection of poems and one of the greatest books ever written. *Wuthering Heights* is surely the most beautiful and most profoundly violent love story. For though Emily Brontë, despite her beauty, appears to have had no experience of love, she had an anguished knowledge of passion. She had the sort of knowledge which links love not only with clarity, but also with violence and death – because death seems to be the truth of love, just as love is the truth of death.

EROTICISM IS THE APPROVAL OF LIFE UP UNTIL DEATH

If I discuss Emily Brontë, I must carry a basic premise to its logical conclusion. I believe eroticism to be the approval of life, up until death. Sexuality implies death, not only in the sense in which the new prolongs and replaces that which has disappeared, but also in that the life of the being who reproduces himself is at stake. To reproduce oneself is to disappear, and even the most basic asexualised being is rarefied by reproduction. Those who reproduce them-selves do not die if, by death, we understand the passage from life to decomposition, but he who was, by reproducing himself, ceases to be what he was – because he doubles himself. Individual death is but one aspect of the proliferative excess of being. Sexual reproduction itself is only one aspect – the most complicated – of the immortality of life which is at stake in asexualised reproduction. It is an aspect of immortality, but at the same time of individual death. No animal can reproduce sexually without yielding to that instinct whose ultimate expression is death. The basis of sexual effusion is the negation of the isolation of the ego which only experiences ecstasy by exceeding itself, by surpassing itself in the embrace in which the being loses its solitude. Whether it is a matter of pure eroticism (love-passion) or of bodily sensuality, the intensity increases to the point where destruction, the death of the being, becomes apparent. What we call vice is based on this profound implication of death. And the anguish of pure love is all the more symbolic of the ultimate truth of love as the death of those whom it unites approaches them and strikes them.

To no mortal love does this apply as much as to the union between the heroes of *Wuthering Heights*, Catherine Earnshaw and Heathcliff. Nobody revealed this truth more forcefully than Emily Brontë. It is not that she envisaged it in the explicit and cumbersome terms in which I have interpreted it: she felt it and expressed it *mortally*, almost divinely.

CHILDHOOD, REASON AND EVIL

The mortal inspiration of *Wuthering Heights* is so powerful that I think it would be pointless to discuss it without attempting to exhaust the question which it raises. I compared vice (which was – and which is still considered to be – the significant expression of Evil) with the anguish of the purest love. This paradoxical comparison lends itself to considerable confusion, so I shall try to justify it.

Though the love of Catherine and Heathcliff leaves sensuality in suspension, *Wuthering Heights* does in fact raise the question of Evil with regard to passion, as if Evil were the most powerful means of exposing passion. If we except the sadistic form of vice, we may say that Evil, as it appears in Emily Brontë's book, has reached its most perfect form.

We cannot consider that actions performed for a material benefit express Evil. This benefit is, no doubt, selfish, but it loses its importance if we expect something from it other than Evil itself – if, for example, we expect some advantage from it. The sadist, on the other hand, obtains pleasure from contemplating destruction, the most complete destruction being the death of another human being. Sadism is Evil. If a man kills for a material advantage his crime only really becomes a purely evil deed if he actually enjoys committing it, independently of the advantage to be obtained from it.

In order to give a better representation of Good and Evil I shall return to the fundamental theme of *Wuthering Heights*, to childhood, when the love between Catherine and Heathcliff originated. The two children spent their time racing wildly on the heath. They abandoned themselves, untrammelled by any restraint or convention other than a taboo on games of sensuality. But, in their innocence, they placed their indestructible love for one another on another level, and indeed perhaps this love can be reduced to the refusal to give up an infantile freedom which had not been amended by the laws of society or of conventional politeness. They led their wild life, outside the world, in the most elementary conditions, and it is these conditions which Emily Brontë made tangible – the basic conditions of poetry, of a spontaneous poetry before which both children refused to stop.

But society contrasts the free play of innocence with reason, reason based on the calculations of interest. Society is governed by its will to survive. It could not survive if these childish instincts, which bound the children in a feeling of complicity, were allowed to triumph. Social constraint would have required the young savages to give up their innocent sovereignty; it would have required them to comply with those reasonable adult conventions which are advantageous to the community.

. This opposition is of primary importance in *Wuthering Heights*. As Jacques Blondel pointed out,[1] we must always keep in mind that 'the feelings are formed during Catherine's and Heathcliff's childhood'. But even if children have the power to forget the world of adults for a time, they are nevertheless doomed to live in this world. Catastrophe ensues. Heathcliff, the foundling, is obliged to flee from the enchanted kingdom where he raced Catherine on the heath, while Catherine, though she remains as rugged as ever, denies her wild childhood: she allows herself to be seduced by the easy life personified by a young, rich and sensitive gentleman. Her marriage with Edgar Linton does, admittedly, retain an element of ambiguity. It is not a true decline. The world of Thrushcross Grange, where Catherine lives with Linton near Wuthering Heights, is far from being a sedentary world in Emily Brontë's eyes. Linton is a generous man. He has not lost the natural pride of youth, but he is settling down. His sovereignty goes beyond the material conditions from which he benefits, but if he were not in profound agreement with the well-established world of reason, he could not benefit from it. So, when he returns rich from a long journey, Heathcliff is prepared to believe that Catherine has betrayed the sovereign kingdom of childhood to which, body and soul, she *belonged* with him.

This, then, is a somewhat clumsy synopsis of a story in which Heathcliff's unbridled violence is recounted calmly and simply. The subject of the book is the revolt of the man accursed, whom fate has banished from his kingdom and who will stop at nothing to regain it. I have no intention of giving a detailed account of a series of fascinating episodes. I am simply going to recall that there is no law or force, no convention or restraining pity which can curb Heathcliff's fury for a single instant – not even death itself, for he is the remorseless and passionate cause of Catherine's disease and death, though he believes her to be his. For I intend to deal with the moral significance of the revolutionary nature of Emily Brontë's imagination and dreams.

It is the revolt of Evil against Good. Formally it is irrational. What does the kingdom of childhood, which

Heathcliff demoniacally refuses to give up, signify if not the *impossible* and ultimate death? There are two ways to revolt against the real world, dominated as it is by reason and based on the will to survive. The most common and relevant is the rejection of its rationality. It is easy to see that the underlying principle of the real world is not really reason, but reason which has come to terms with that arbitrary element born of the violence and puerile instincts of the past. Such a revolt exposes the struggle of Good against Evil, represented by violence or by puerility. Heathcliff passes judgement on the world to which he is opposed. He cannot identify it with Good because he is fighting it. But even if he is fighting it furiously, he is doing so lucidly: he knows that he represents Good and reason. He hates the humanity and goodness which provoke his sarcasm. If we imagine him outside the story, bereft of the charm of the story, his character seems artificial and contrived. But he is conceived in the dreams, not the logic, of the author. There is no character in romantic literature who comes across more convincingly or more simply than Heathcliff, although he represents a very basic state – that of the child in revolt against the world of Good, against the adult world, and committed, in his revolt, to the side of Evil.

In this revolt there is no law which Heathcliff does not enjoy breaking. He sees that Catherine's sister-in-law is in love with him, so he marries her in order to do Catherine's husband as much harm as he can. He abducts her and, as soon as they are married, scorns her. He then proceeds to drive her to despair by his callous treatment of her. Jacques Blondel[2] is right to compare the following two passages from Sade and Emily Brontë: 'How sensual is the act of destruction,' says one of the executioners in *Justine*, 'I can think of nothing which excites me more deliciously. There is no ecstasy similar to that which we experience when we yield to this divine infamy.' 'Had I been born where laws are less strict and tastes less dainty,' says Heathcliff, 'I should treat myself to a slow vivisection of those two, as an evening's amusement.'

EMILY BRONTË AND TRANSGRESSION

The mere invention of a character so totally devoted to Evil by a moral and inexperienced girl would be a paradox. But the invention of Heathcliff is particularly worrying for the following reasons: Catherine Earnshaw herself is absolutely moral. She is so moral that she dies of not being able to detach herself from the man she loved when she was a child. But although she knows that Evil is deep within him, she loves him to the point of saying 'I am Heathcliff'.

Evil, therefore, if we examine it closely, is not only the dream of the wicked: it is to some extent the dream of Good. Death is the punishment, sought and accepted for this mad dream, but nothing can prevent the dream from having been dreamt. It was dreamt by the unfortunate Catherine Earnshaw as well as by Emily Brontë. How can we doubt that Emily Brontë, who died for having experienced the states of mind which she described, identified herself with Catherine Earnshaw?

Wuthering Heights has a certain affinity with Greek tragedy. The subject of the novel is the tragic violation of the law. The tragic author agreed with the law, the transgression of which he described, but he based all emotional impact on communicating the sympathy which he felt for the transgressor. In both cases atonement is connected with transgression. Before he dies and as he dies, Heathcliff experiences a curious state of beatitude, but this beatitude has something terrifying about it: it is tragic. Catherine, who loves Heathcliff, dies for having broken the laws of fidelity – not in the flesh but in the spirit. And Catherine's death is the perpetual agony which Heathcliff suffers for his violence.

In *Wuthering Heights*, as in Greek tragedy, it is not the law itself that is denounced: what it forbids is simply described as an essentially human domain, made for man. The forbidden domain is the tragic domain or, better still, the sacred domain. Humanity, admittedly, banishes it, but only in order to magnify it, and the ban beautifies that to which it prevents access. It subordinates access to atonement – to death. Yet the ban is no less an invitation at the same time as it is an obstacle. The lesson of *Wuthering Heights*, of Greek tragedy and, ultimately, of all religions, is that there is an instinctive tendency towards divine intoxication which the rational world of calculation cannot bear. This tendency is the opposite of Good. Good is based on common interest which entails consideration of the future. Divine intoxication, to which the instincts of childhood are so closely related, is entirely in the present. In the education of children preference for the present moment is the common definition of Evil. Adults forbid those who have still to reach 'maturity' to enter the divine kingdom of childhood. But condemnation of the present moment for the sake of the future is an aberration. Just as it is necessary to forbid easy access to it, so it is necessary to regain the domain of the moment (the kingdom of childhood), and that requires temporary transgression of the interdict.

Such temporary transgression is all the more free since the interdict is considered intangible. So Emily Brontë and Catherine Earnshaw, who both appear to us in the light of transgression and atonement, depend less on morality than on hypermorality. Hypermorality is the basis of that challenge to morality which is fundamental to *Wuthering Heights*. Though he does not actually refer to the principle I gave developed, Blondel has sensed the connection. He writes:[3]

> Emily Brontë shows herself... capable of emancipating herself from all prejudice of an ethical or social order. Thus several lives develop... each of which conveys a sense of total liberation from society and morality. There is a desire to break with the world in order to embrace life in all its fullness and discover in artistic creativity that which is refused by reality. This is the revelation, or rather the inauguration, of hitherto unsuspected potentialities. That this liberation is necessary to every artist is certain; and *it can be felt most intensely by those in whom ethical values are most deeply rooted.*[4]

This intimate connection between the transgression of the moral law and hypermorality is the ultimate meaning of *Wuthering Heights*. Elsewhere[5] Jacques Blondel describes the religious atmosphere: Protestantism influenced by the recollection of an exalted type of Methodism, in which the young Emily Brontë was brought up. Her world was crushed by moral tension and severity. Yet Emily Brontë's form of severity differs from that on which Greek tragedy was based. Tragedy is on a level with the basic religious taboos, like those forbidding murder and incest, which cannot be justified rationally. Emily Brontë had emancipated herself from orthodoxy: she had moved away from Christian simplicity and innocence, but she participated in the religious spirit of her family to the extent in which Christianity is strict fidelity to Good based on reason. The law violated by Heathcliff – and which Catherine also violates by loving him in spite of herself – is the law of reason. It is, at least, the law of a community founded by Christianity on an alliance between primitive religious taboos, holiness and reason.[6] In Christianity God, the underlying principle of holiness, partially escapes from the arbitrary violence on which the divine world was based in ancient times. The primitive taboo was essentially directed against violence – in practice reason fulfils the same purpose as the taboo, while the primitive taboo itself has a distant relationship with reason. There is, in Christianity, an ambivalence where God and reason are concerned which has given rise to a feeling of unease and such subsidiary phenomena as Jansenism. After this long drawn-out Christian ambivalence, what suddenly comes to light in Emily Brontë's attitude, by means of an intangible moral solidity, is the dream of a sacred violence which no settlement with organised society can attenuate.

The road to the kingdom of childhood, governed by ingenuousness and innocence, is thus regained *in the horror of atonement*. The purity of love is regained in its intimate truth which, as I said, is that of death. Death and the instant of divine intoxication merge when they both oppose those intentions of Good which are based on rational calculation. And death indicates the instant which, in so far as it is instantaneous, renounces the calculated quest for survival. The instant of the new individual being depended on the death of other beings. Had they not died there would have been no room for new ones. Reproduction and death condition the immortal renewal of life; they condition the instant which is always new. That is why we can only have a tragic view of the enchantment of life, but that is also why tragedy is the symbol of enchantment. The entire romantic movement may have heralded this,[7] but that late masterpiece, *Wuthering Heights*, heralds it most humanely.

LITERATURE, LIBERTY AND THE MYSTICAL EXPERIENCE

The most remarkable thing about this movement is that its doctrine, unlike that of Christianity or of the ancient religions, is not aimed at an organised community of which it would be the foundation. It is aimed at the isolated and lost individual to whom it gives nothing except in this one instant: it is solely literature. The path towards literature, free and inorganic, leads towards it. For this reason it falls behind the teaching of the pagan sages or of the Church, which has to come to terms with social necessity represented, in most cases, by conventions (abuses) as well as by reason. Only literature could reveal the process of breaking the law – without which the law would have no end – *independently of the necessity to create order*. Literature cannot assume the task of regulating collective necessity. It should not conclude that 'what I have said commits us to a fundamental respect for the laws of the city' or, like Christianity, that 'what I have said (the tragedy of the Gospel) shows us the path of Good' (which is really the path of reason). Literature, like the infringement of moral laws, is dangerous.

Being inorganic, it is irresponsible. Nothing rests on it. It can say everything and would be a great danger (to the extent in which it is authentic and complete) were it not the expression of 'those in whom ethical values are most deeply rooted'. Though the immediate impression of rebellion may obscure this fact, the task of authentic literature is nevertheless only conceivable in terms of a desire for a fundamental communication with the reader. (I do not, of course, refer to the mass of books designed to put a great many people on the wrong scent.)

Literature, connected since romanticism with the decadence of religion in that it tends to lay a discreet claim to the heritage of religion, is not so much cognate with the content of religion as it is with the content of mysticism which, incidentally, is an almost asocial aspect of religion. Similarly mysticism is closer to the truth than I can possibly say. By mysticism I do not mean those systems of thought on which this vague name is conferred. I refer, rather, to the 'mystical experience', to those 'mystical states' experienced in solitude. In these states we can see a different truth to that which is concerned with the perception of objects, or indeed of the subject, connected, as it is, with the intellectual consequences of perception. But this is not a formal truth. Coherent discussion cannot account for it. It would be incommunicable if we could not approach it in two ways: through poetry and through the description of those conditions by which one arrives at these states.

These conditions correspond decisively with the themes which I have mentioned and which constitute the basis of true literary emotion. Death alone – or, at least, the ruin of the isolated individual in search of happiness in time – introduces that break without which nothing reaches the state of ecstasy.[8] And what we thereby regain is always both innocence and the intoxication of existence. The isolated being *loses himself* in something other than himself. What the 'other thing' represents is of no importance. It is still a reality that transcends the common limitations. So unlimited is it that it is not even a thing: it is *nothing*.

'God is nothingness', said Eckhart. In everyday life it is surely the 'loved one' himself who is the removal of the limitations of others – he is the only being in whom we no longer feel, or in whom we are less aware of, those limitations of the individual confined within that isolation which is in itself a defect. The mystical state is characterised by a tendency to suppress, radically and systematically, that multiple image of the world in which one finds the individual existence in search of survival. With a sudden impulse (as in childhood or passion) the effort ceases to be systematic: the limitations are broken passively, not by intense intellectual will power. The image of this world is merely incoherent, or, if it has already found its cohesion, the intensity of passion exceeds it. It is true that passion seeks to prolong the enjoyment experienced in the loss of the self, but surely it starts with the obliteration of one self by the other. We cannot doubt the fundamental unity of all those instincts by which we escape from the calculations of interest and in which we feel the intensity of the present moment. Mysticism is as far from the spontaneity of childhood as it is from the accidental condition of passion. But it expresses its trances through the vocabulary of love. And contemplation liberated from discursive reflection has the simplicity of a child's laugh.

I believe it is essential to stress those aspects which the modern literary tradition and mysticism have in common. And indeed the similarity is striking as far as Emily Brontë is concerned. In his recent study Jacques Blondel speaks of her mystical *experience* as though Emily Brontë had exerienced the visions and the ecstasy of Teresa of Avila. But Blondel probably goes too far. There is no evidence, there is no positive support for an interpretation which he, in fact, does no more than enlarge upon. Others before him have sensed a connection between the spiritual states of a Saint Teresa and those which Emily Brontë expressed in her poetry. Nevertheless, it is doubtful whether the author of *Wuthering Heights* was acquainted with that methodical descent into the self which serves as the basic definition of a *mystical experience*.

Jacques Blondel quotes a number of passages from her poems. They do indeed describe certain acute feelings and troubled states of mind which suggest an anguished spiritual life brought to the point of intense exaltation. They express an infinitely profound, infinitely violent experience of sadness or of the joys of solitude. Admittedly nothing entitles us to distinguish such an experience from a more systematic quest, subjected to the principles of religion or of a certain representation of the world, positive or negative. We might almost say that these stray impulses, regulated by chance and always attributable to rambling reflection, are sometimes the richest of all. The imprecise world which the poems reveal to us is immense and bewildering. But we should beware of equating it too closely with the relatively familiar world described by the great mystics. It is less calm, more savage. Its violence is not slowly reabsorbed in the gradual experience of an enlightenment. It is, in short, far closer to the indescribable anguish expressed in *Wuthering Heights*.

> Yet I would lose no sting, would wish no torture
> less;
> The more that anguish racks, the earlier it will
> bless;
> And robed in fires of hell, or bright with heavenly
> shine,
> If it but herald death, the vision is divine!

In my opinion these lines from *The Prisoner* are the most powerful example of that feeling which underlies Emily Brontë's poetry. They convey her state of mind, admirably.

Finally it matters little whether Emily Brontë really had what we call a mystical experience, for she appears to have reached the very essence of such an experience.

'Everything leads us to believe,' wrote André Breton,[9] 'that there is a certain point in the mind where life and death, the real and the imaginary, the past and the future, the communicable and the incommunicable, are no longer perceived in contradiction to one another.' I shall add: Good and Evil, pain and joy. This point is indicated both by violent literature and by the violence of a mystical experience: only the point matters.

Yet it is also important to realise that *Wuthering Heights*, the most violent and most poetic of Emily Brontë's works, is the name of a 'high place' where truth is revealed. It is the name of an accursed house, damned by Heathcliff as he enters it. By a striking paradox, 'the beings perish' once they are far away from this accursed place.[10] And indeed, the violence introduced by Heathcliff is the basis both of a misery and of a happiness which only 'enchant the violent'. The end of Emily Brontë's sombre tale is the sudden appearance of a faint ray of light.

In so far as violence casts its shadow on the being and he sees death 'face to face', life is purely beneficial. Nothing can destroy it. Death is the condition of its renewal.

THE SIGNIFICANCE OF EVIL

In this union of opposites, Evil is no longer as irrevocably opposed to the natural order as it exists within the limitations of reason. Since death is the condition of life, Evil, which is essentially cognate with death, is also, in a somewhat ambiguous manner, a basis of existence. Though the being is not doomed to Evil, he must try to avoid becoming enclosed within the limitations of reason. He must first accept these limitations and acknowledge the necessity of calculated interest, but he must also know that an irreducible, sovereign part of himself is free from the limitations and the necessity which he acknowledges.

In as far as it expresses an attraction towards death, and in as far as it is a challenge which exists in all forms of eroticism, Evil is always the object of an ambiguous condemnation. It can be glorious, as it is, for all its horrors, in war. But war has imperialism as its consequence... It would be pointless to deny that Evil always contains a potential tendency to become worse, and it is this that justifies anguish and disgust. But it is no less true to say that Evil, seen in the light of a disinterested attraction towards death, differs from the evil based on self-interest. A 'foul' criminal deed is contrary to a 'passionate' one. The law rejects both of them, but truly humane literature is the high point of passion. Yet passion does not go without a curse: only a 'cursed share' is set aside for that part of human life which has the greatest significance.[11] The curse is the necessary path for true blessing.

An honourable human being *loyally* accepts the worst consequences of his challenge. Sometimes he even goes out to meet them. The 'cursed share' is the gamble, the risk, the danger. It is also sovereignty, but sovereignty must be expiated. The world of *Wuthering Heights* is the world of a hostile sovereignty. It is also the world of expiation. Once the expiation has been accepted, the true smile of life appears.

NOTES

1. Jacques Blondel, *Emily Brontë. Expérience spirituelle et création poétique* P.U.F., 1955.
2. Ibid.
3. Ibid.
4. My italics.
5. Op. cit.
6. There can be no doubt that, within the limits of Christianity, reason comes to terms with those social conventions which express some form of abuse.
7. Jacques Blondel has emphasised Emily Brontë's debt to romanticism and, more particularly, to Byron, whom she certainly read.
8. Christian mysticism is based on 'death to the self'. Oriental mysticism has the same basis. 'In India,' wrote Mircea Eliade, 'metaphysical knowledge expresses itself in terms of a break and of death... [and] this knowledge implies... a mystical succession... The yogee tries to detach himself from the profane condition... he dreams of "dying to this life". Indeed, we see a *death* followed by a *rebirth*, another way of being – the way of being which is deliverance.' *'Yoga, Immortality and Freedom.*
9. *Les Manifestes du surrealism.* 'Second Manifeste' (1930).
10. J. Blondel, op. cit.
11. In *La Part maudite*, Editions de Minuit, 1949, I attempted to trace this view in religious and economic history.

BAUDELAIRE

MAN CANNOT LOVE HIMSELF TO THE END UNLESS HE CONDEMNS HIMSELF

Sartre has defined Baudelaire's moral position with the utmost precision.[1]

> To do Evil for the sake of Evil is to do the exact opposite of what we continue to affirm is Good. It is to want what we do not want – since we continue to abhor the powers of Evil – and not to want what we want, for Good is always defined as the object and end of the deepest will. This was Baudelaire's attitude. Between his acts and those of the normal sinner there lay the same difference as between black magic and atheism. The atheist does not care about God because he has decided once and for all that He does not exist. But the priest of the black mass hates God because He is lovable; he scorns Him because He is respectable; he sets himself to denying the established order, but, at the same time, preserves this order and asserts it more than ever. Were he for a moment to stop asserting it his conscience would return to peace with itself. Evil would suddenly turn into Good and, transcending all orders which do not emanate from himself, he would emerge in nothingness, without God, without excuses, having assumed his full responsibility.

This is undoubtedly true. Further on, Sartre's view is of still greater interest.

> In order for liberty to be complete it has to be offered the choice... of being infinitely wrong. It is therefore *unique* in this whole universe committed to Good, but it must adhere totally to Good, maintain it and strengthen it in order to be able to plunge into Evil. And he who damns himself acquires a solitude which is a feeble image of the great solitude of the truly free man. In a certain sense he creates. In a universe where each element sacrifices itself in order to converge in the greatness of the whole, he brings out the singularity, that is to say the rebelliousness of a fragment or a detail. Thus something appears which did not exist before, which nothing can efface and which was in no way prepared by worldly materialism. It becomes a work of luxury, gratuitous and unpredictable. Let us observe the relationship between Evil and poetry: when poetry goes as far as to take Evil as its object the two forms of creation, whose responsibility is essentially limited, meet and merge – we possess a flower of Evil. But the deliberate creation of Evil – that is to say, wrong – is acceptance and recognition of Good. It pays homage to it and, by calling itself wicked, it admits that it is relative and derivative – that it could not exist without Good.

Sartre also refers, in passing, to the relationship between Evil and poetry, but he draws no conclusions from it. The evil element is very apparent in Baudelaire's work, but is it connected with the essential nature of poetry? Sartre says nothing about this. He merely describes as liberty that possible state in which man is no longer supported by traditional Good – or by the established order. In comparison to this major position, he regards the poet's position as minor. Baudelaire 'never went beyond the phase of childhood'. 'He defined genius as "childhood regained at will".'[2] Childhood lives in faith.

> But if the child grows older, grows superior to his parents in intelligence and looks over their shoulder, (he may see that) behind them there is nothing.[3] The duties, the rites, the precise and limited obligations suddenly disappear. Unjustified and unjustifiable, he suddenly experiences his terrible liberty. Everything has to be begun again: he suddenly emerges in solitude and nothingness. That was what Baudelaire wanted to avoid at all costs.[4]

At one point in his study[5] Sartre reproaches Baudelaire for having regarded 'moral life as a constraint . . . and never as a tortured quest'. But surely we can say of poetry – and not only of Baudelaire's poetry – that it is a 'tortured quest' for a moral truth which it may have discovered by mistake? Sartre has unintentionally connected the ethical problem with the poetic problem. He quotes a passage from Baudelaire's letter to Ancelle, dated 18 February, 1866. 'Should I tell you, who have guessed it no more than the others, that I have put my whole heart, my whole affection, my whole religion (in disguise), my whole hatred, my whole misfortune into this atrocious book? It is true that I will write the contrary, that I will swear by the gods that it is a book of pure art, of imitation, of imposture, and I will be an arrant liar.' Sartre includes this quotation[6] in his proof that Baudelaire acknowledged the ethics of his judges and made *Les Fleurs du Mal* pass for a diversion (a work of Art for Art's sake) or for 'an edifying work intended to instil in the reader a horror for vice'. The letter to Ancelle undoubtedly makes better sense than the disguises. But Sartre has simplified a problem which calls into question the very basis of poetry and ethics.

If liberty – I must be allowed to state my proposition before I justify it – is the essential quality of poetry, and if free and sovereign behaviour deserves no more than a 'tortured quest', the misery of poetry and the bonds imposed by liberty become evident. Though poetry may trample verbally on the established order, it is no substitute for it. When disgust with a powerless liberty thoroughly commits the poet to political action he abandons poetry. But he immediately assumes responsibility for the order to come: he asserts the direction of activity, the major attitude. When we see him we cannot help being aware that poetic existence, in which we once saw the possibility of a sovereign attitude, is really a minor attitude. It becomes no more than a child's attitude, a gratuitous game. Strictly speaking liberty would be the power of a child. For the adult, bound by the obligatory regulations of action, it would be a mere dream, a desire, a spectre. Is liberty not the power which God lacks, or which He only possesses verbally since He cannot disobey the order which *He is*, which He guarantees?

God's profound liberty disappears for the man in whose eyes Satan alone is free. 'But who, basically, is Satan?' asks Sartre,[7] 'if not the symbol of disobedient and sulky children who want to remain as their parents see them and who do Evil within the bounds of Good in order to assert and consecrate it?' The liberty of the child (or the devil) is evidently limited by the adult (or by God), who turns it to mockery (who diminishes it). The child, therefore, nurtures feelings of hatred and rebelliousness restrained by admiration and envy. In so far as he approaches rebellion he assumes an adult's responsibility. He can, if he likes, blind himself in various ways. He can pretend to assume the major prerogatives of the adult, but without acknowledging the obligations connected with them – this would be the ingenuous attitude, the bluff which requires complete puerility. He can continue to lead a free life at the expense of those who are entertained by him – this limp form of liberty is traditionally the poet's prerogative. He can put other people off with fine words, or he can alleviate the weight of a prosaic reality by emphasising it. But there is both an air of imposture and an evil odour connected with these poor possibilities. If it is true that the impossible, which has, in a way, been chosen and therefore acknowledged, smells no less foul, and if the ultimate unsatisfaction (that with which the mind is satisfied) is itself a form of imposture, we can at least say that there is a privileged form of misery which admits itself to be such.

It is ashamed to admit itself to be such. The problems which Sartre unwittingly raises cannot easily be solved. If it is true that Baudelaire's attitude was in many ways unfortunate, it seems inhuman to hold it against him. Yet we would have no alternative if we were not to take into account the fact that Baudelaire deliberately refused to behave like a real man, that is to say, like a prosaic man. Sartre is right: Baudelaire chose to be wrong, like a child. But before we condemn him we must ask ourselves what sort of choice we are dealing with. Was it made for lack of anything else? Was it just a deplorable mistake? Or was it the result of excess? Was it made in a miserable but no less decisive manner? I even wonder whether such a choice is not essentially that of poetry? Is it not *the choice of man?*

This is the point of my book. I believe that man is necessarily put up against himself and that he cannot recognise himself and love himself to the end unless he is condemned.

THE PROSAIC WORLD OF ACTIVITY AND THE WORLD OF POETRY

My previous propositions bring us to a world which I cannot blame Sartre for avoiding. My book is an attempt to discover this new world. But this will only appear gradually...

'If man did not shut his eyes in a sovereign manner,' wrote René Char, 'he would end up by no longer seeing things worth looking at.' But, Sartre says[8]

> For the rest of us, it is enough to see the tree or the house. Absorbed as we are in contemplating them, we forget ourselves. Baudelaire was the man who never forgot himself. He watched himself seeing, he watched in order to see himself watching. It was his awareness of the tree or the house which he watched, and things only appeared to him through his awareness, paler, smaller, less touching, as though he saw them through a pair of opera glasses. They did not point to each other like a signpost or a book marker... Their immediate mission was to bring the individual back to self-awareness.[9] [And further on] There was an original distance between Baudelaire and the world, which is not ours. Between the objects and himself there was always a somewhat cloying lucidity, like a breath of warm summer air.

There is no better or more precise way of representing the distance between poetic vision and everyday life. We forget ourselves when the signpost points to the road or the marker shows us the page in a book. But this vision is not *sovereign*: it is subordinate to our search for the road (which we are about to take) or for the page (which we are about to read). In other words the present (the signpost or the book marker) is here determined by the future (the road or the page). According to Sartre,[10] 'it is the determination of the present by the future, of what exists by what does not yet exist... which philosophers today call transcendence.' In as much as the signpost or the book marker have this transcendent significance they do admittedly suppress us and we forget ourselves if we look upon them in this subordinate manner. The 'paler, smaller, less touching' things, on the other hand, to which Baudelaire opened his eyes *sovereignly*, did not suppress him for they served 'no other purpose than to give him the opportunity of observing himself as he saw them.'[11]

I should point out that though Sartre does not actually move away from his object, he errs by allowing a certain confusion to arise. I apologise for entering into a philosophical digression here in order to prove this point.

I shall not discuss the confusion of ideas which induces Sartre to represent the 'things' of Baudelaire's poetic vision as 'less touching' than a signpost or a book marker (we are concerned here with categories: the first that of objects which appeal to our senses, the second that of objects which appeal to practical knowledge). But it is not the signpost and the road which Sartre sees as transcendent (I have had to cut the passage in order to use it)[12]. It is the objects of poetic contemplation. I admit that this conforms with the vocabulary he chooses, but in this case the inadequacy of the vocabulary does not permit us to sustain a real challenge. We are told[13] that Baudelaire wanted 'to find in each reality a fixed unsatisfaction, an appeal to something else, an objective transcendency...' Transcendency thus represented is no longer the simple transcendency of the signpost, the mere 'determination of the present by the future'. It is the transcendency of 'objects which are prepared to suppress themselves in order to point out others.' It is, he specifies[14] 'the goal that has been glimpsed, almost touched, but is still beyond expression...' Admittedly the direction of this 'precisely orientated' expression is determined by the future, but the future, as a direction, is not the accessible road indicated by the signpost. Indeed, the direction of the future is only there in order to elude us.

Or rather it is not the future so much as the spectre of the future. And Sartre himself says that 'its special and irrevocable nature puts us on the right track: the true direction – the direction of those objects spiritualised by the void in which they dissolve – is the *past*.'[15]

I said to begin with that Sartre's passionate verdict demanded nothing less than a punctilious discussion. I would not have embarked on this lengthy elucidation if anything other than an inconsequential confusion were at stake. I have some difficulty in seeing the point of a certain type of polemic: I do not want to level a personal attack, I simply want to ensure the defence of poetry. If I mention a challenge, it is because one must insist on that which poetry puts at stake.

It is obvious that in everything, in the signpost as in the spectral figures of poetry, past, present and future contribute to the determination of the meaning. But the direction in which the signpost is pointing indicates the primacy of the future. At the same time the future only intervenes negatively, in the determination of the direction of poetic objects, by revealing an impossibility and placing the desire before the inevitable unsatisfaction. Finally, if we also realise that the sense of a 'transcendent' object of poetry is also the equality with the self, we cannot help being upset by the imprecision of the vocabulary. We cannot deny that this element of *immanence* has been immediately perceived by Sartre himself who, as we have seen, leads us to understand[16] that the tree and the house represented by Baudelaire served 'no other purpose than to give [the poet] the opportunity of *observing himself*.' At this point I feel I should emphasise the value of 'mystical participation', of identification of the subject with the object which it is in the power of poetry to express. It is curious to observe that within a few lines Sartre passes from 'an objectivised transcendency' to 'this hierarchical order of objects which are prepared *to lose themselves* in order to indicate others', where 'Baudelaire recovers *his image.*'[17] The essence of Baudelaire's poetry is to affect, at the cost of an agonising tension, the fusion between the subject (immanence) and those objects which lose themselves both in order to cause anguish and to reflect it.

Having defined transcendence as the determination of the present by the future, Sartre considers those objects transcendent whose sense is provided by the past and whose essence is to be in a relationship of immanence with the subject. There would be nothing wrong with this (we shall soon see that the ambivalence is partly that of the things envisaged), if we did not lose, in the course of these transpositions, the possibility of clearly presenting the fundamental distinction between the prosaic world of activity – where the objects which are clearly extrinsic to the subject have a fundamental sense of the future (it is the road that determines the direction of the signpost) – and the world of poetry. We can define poetics – similar in this to Lévy-Bruhl's primitivity and to Piaget's puerility – by a subject-object relationship. Participation is of the present moment. No allowance for the future will help us to determine it, any more than, in primitive magic, it is the outcome which gives meaning to the operation. Indeed, in order for primitive magic to work, it must above all contain a true sense of participation, independent of the outcome. The operation of the signpost, on the other hand, has no other sense as far as the subject is concerned than that of the future, the road to which it leads. Nor is the sense of the object in poetic participation determined by the past. Only an object of memory, bereft both of use and of poetry, would be the pure *donnée* of the past. In the poetic process the sense of objects of memory is determined by the *present* invasion of the subject. We must keep in mind the etymological connotation according to which poetry is creation. The fusion of object and subject requires the transcendence of each party as soon as it enters into contact with the other. Only the possibility of pure repetition prevents us from perceiving the primacy of the present. We must even go so far as to say that poetry never represents regret for the past. Only regret which lies is poetic. It ceases to be true to the extent in which it becomes true, for the past is of less interest in the object of regret than the expression of regret.

These suggestions lead us back to Sartre's analysis (from which I have only diverged in order to emphasise its profundity). If it is true that the poetic process wants the object to become the subject, the subject the object, would it be more than a game, a brilliant sleight of hand? Basically there can be no doubt about the possibility of poetry. But is the history of poetry a mere succession of futile efforts? We can hardly deny that, as a general rule, poets cheat! 'Poets lie too much,' says Zarathustra, who adds 'Zarathustra himself is a poet'. But the fusion of subject and object, of man and the world, cannot be feigned. We could avoid attempting it in the first place, but that would be absurd.

Such a fusion would appear to be impossible. Sartre rightly says, with regard to this impossibility, that the tragedy of the poet is due to the mad desire to unite the being and existence objectively. I have already said that, according to Sartre, this desire is, at times, that of Baudelaire in particular, and at others, that of 'every poet'. But whichever way we look at it the synthesis of the unchangeable and the perishable, of the being and existence, of the object and the subject, which poetry seeks, is an ultimate definition of poetry. It limits it and transposes it into the realm of the impossible and the unsatisfiable. Unfortunately it is difficult to talk of the impossible being condemned to existence. The recurrent theme of Sartre's study is that Baudelaire's misfortune was to want to be what he was for others: he thereby abandoned the prerogative of existence, which is to remain in abeyance. But does man tend to prevent his consciousness from becoming a thing like any other by letting it become a reflection of things? I do not think so. Poetry is the means by which, in his ignorance of the means Sartre has proposed to him, he can escape from being reduced to the reflection of things. It is true that poetry, in its quest for the identity of reflected things and the consciousness which reflects them, wants the impossible. But surely the very means of avoiding reduction to the reflection of things constitute a desire for the impossible.

IN A SENSE POETRY IS ALWAYS THE OPPOSITE OF POETRY

I believe that the misery of poetry is faithfully represented in Sartre's image of Baudelaire. There is, inherent in poetry, an obligation to turn unsatisfaction into a permanent object. In a first impulse poetry destroys the objects which it seizes. By destroying them it returns them to the elusive fluidity of the poet's existence and it is at this point that it hopes to regain the identity of the world and man. But at the same time as it releases the objects, it tries to seize this release. All it can do is substitute the release for what it has seized from reduced life: it can never allow the release to take the place of the objects it once seized.

Here we are confronted with a difficulty similar to that of the child who is free to deny the adult, but who cannot do so without becoming an adult in his turn, and thereby forfeiting his freedom. But Baudelaire, who never assumed the prerogatives of the masters, and whose liberty guaranteed his insatiability to the end, nevertheless had to rival these beings whom he had refused to replace. Admittedly he searched for himself, never lost or forgot himself, and watched himself watching. The recuperation of being was, as Sartre indicated, the object of his genius, his tension and his poetic impotence. There can be no doubt that at the origin of the poet's destiny there is a certainty of uniqueness, of election, without which the task of reducing the world to oneself or of losing oneself in the world would lose its significance. Sartre makes this Baudelaire's defect. He attributes it to the isolation in which he was left by his mother's second marriage. This is indeed the 'feeling of solitude since my childhood', 'or an eternally solitary destiny' of which the poet himself spoke. But Baudelaire undoubtedly gave just as valid a revelation of himself when he said: 'As a child I felt in my heart two contradictory feelings, the horror of life and the ecstasy of life.' We cannot sufficiently emphasise the certainty of irreplaceable uniqueness which is at the basis not only of poetic genius (Blake saw this as the common denominator which made poets similar to all men), but of every religion (of each Church) and of every country. It is quite true that poetry has always corresponded to the desire to recuperate, to mould in a tangible, external form a unique existence which was first unformed and which would otherwise only have been palpable within something, within an individual or a group. But it is doubtful whether our awareness of existing does not necessarily have that deceptive quality of uniqueness: the individual may feel it by belonging to a city, a family or even a couple (according to Sartre Baudelaire experienced this as a child, bound body and heart to his mother), or he may feel it on his own account. Nowadays, no doubt, it is this latter case which brings about poetic vocations and which leads to a form of verbal creativity in which the poem is the recuperation of the individual. We could thus say that the poet is the part taking itself for the whole, the individual behaving like the community.

So states of unsatisfaction, objects which deceive or which reveal an absence, are the only forms through which the individual recovers his deceptive uniqueness. The city might fix it or establish it, but isolated existence alone has the chance to do what the city must and can do, without the power to do it. It is all very well for Sartre to say of Baudelaire:[18] 'his dearest wish was to *be* like the stone, the statue, in the repose of immutability.' He can represent the poet as eager to extract some petrifiable image from the mists of the past, but the images which he left participated in a life which was open, infinite in Baudelaire's sense of the word,[19] that is to say, unsatisfied. It is therefore misleading to maintain that Baudelaire wanted the impossible statue or that he could not exist, unless we immediately add that he wanted the impossible far more than he wanted the statue.

It would be more reasonable – and less contemptuous – to examine in this light the feeling of uniqueness or of awareness which Baudelaire had as a child, believing that he alone was the ecstasy and the horror of life and that nothing would alleviate its weight. We must examine all the consequences of 'this miserable life'. Sartre is justified in claiming that Baudelaire *wanted* something which seems ruinous to us. At least he wanted it as one wants the *impossible* – that is to say both genuinely as such, and deceptively, in the form of a chimera. Hence his tortured existence as a dandy, longing for work but bitterly engulfed in a useless idleness. But since, as Sartre admits, he was armed with 'incomparable tension', he drew all he could from an untenable position. A perfect expression of ecstasy and horror gave his poetry a fullness sustained *to the very limits* of a free sensibility,[20] an exhaustive form of rarefaction and sterility which makes Sartre uneasy. The atmosphere of vice, rejection and hatred correspond to the tension of the will which denied the constraint of Good in the same way as the athlete denies the weight of the dumb-bell. It is true that every effort is fruitless. The poems in which this expression is petrified and which reduce existence to being, have made of *infinite* vice, hatred and liberty those tranquil, docile and immutable forms with which we are acquainted. It is also true that poetry which survives is always the opposite of poetry for, having the perishable as its subject, it transforms it into something eternal. But it matters little if poetry, whose essential nature is to unite the object of the poem with the subject, unites it with the poet, disappointed, unsatisfied and humiliated by failure. The object, the world, irreducible and unsubordinated, incarnated in the hybrid creation of poetry and betrayed by the poem, is not betrayed by the poet's unlivable life. Only the poet's interminable agony can really reveal the authenticity of poetry, and Sartre, whatever he may say, helps us to see that Baudelaire's end, preceding the glory which alone could have changed him to stone, corresponded to his will: *Baudelaire wanted the impossible until the end.*

BAUDELAIRE AND THE STATUE OF THE IMPOSSIBLE

A little discernment in the awareness of our own reality justifies hesitation. We cannot know 'distinctly' what had supreme value for Baudelaire. Perhaps we should deduce some indication of the fatal relationship between man and value from the very fact that he chose to ignore it. We may betray what has supreme value for us if we have the weakness to decide about it 'distinctly'. There is nothing surprising in liberty demanding a leap, a sudden and unforeseeable snatch, no longer accorded to those who decide in advance. It is true that Baudelaire remained a maze for himself. Leaving every possibility open in every direction until the end, he aspired to the immutability of stone, the onanism of a funereal poem. We cannot help perceiving a permanence of the past within him, an exhaustion heralding inertia, a precocious old age, impotence. In *Les Fleurs du Mal* we find grounds for justifying Sartre's interpretation according to which Baudelaire made sure that he was only an 'unchangeable and imperfectible' past and chose 'to consider his life from the standpoint of death, as if a premature end had already fixed it.'

The fullness of his poetry may be connected with the immobilised image of the trapped animal which he gave of himself, which obsessed him, which he continually evoked, just as a nation resolves to live up to the image it once had of itself and agrees to disappear rather than to fail it. Creativity which receives its limitations from the past comes to a halt. Because it has a feeling of unsatisfaction, it cannot detach itself and is content to live in a state of permanent unsatisfaction. This morose pleasure, prolonged by failure, this terror of being satisfied, changes liberty into its opposite. But Sartre stresses the fact that Baudelaire's life was played out in a few years and that, after the outburst of youth, it slowed down to an interminable decline. He writes:

By 1846, [that is to say when Baudelaire was twenty-five] he had spent half his fortune, written most of his poems, given a definitive form to his relationship with his parents, contracted the venereal disease which was slowly going to kill him. He had met the woman who was to weigh like lead on every hour of his life, and he had accomplished the journey which was to furnish his work with exotic images.[21]

But this view leads us to Sartre's opinion of the *Ecrits Intimes*. They are repetitions, and they distress him. I would like to dwell on a letter dated January 28, 1854.[22] In it

Baudelaire gives the outline of a play. In a deserted spot at night a drunken workman meets the woman who has abandoned him. She refuses to return home with him, despite his pleas. In despair he leads her along a footpath, knowing that she will fall into a well. The episode originates with a song. 'It begins,' he wrote, 'by:

Rien n'est aussi-z-aimable
Franfru-Cancru-Lon-La-Lahira
Rien n'est aussi-z-aimable
Que le scieur de long.

... Finally, this amiable sawyer throws his wife into the water. He then addresses a Siren...

Chantre Sirène Chante
Franfru-Cancru-Lon-La-Lahira
Chante Sirène Chante
T'as raison de chanter.

Car t'as la mer à boire,
Franfru-Cancru-Lon-La-Lahira
Car t'as la mer à boire,
Et ma mie à manger.'

The sawyer is burdened with the author's sins; by way of a change of key – a masque – the image of the poet suddenly thaws. It is deformed and changes. It ceases to be the image determined by a rigid rhythm, so tense that it moulds things in advance.[23] The limited past no longer casts a spell. An unlimited possibility reveals the attraction which pertains to it – the attraction of liberty, of the rejection of limitation. It was not purely by chance that the theme of the sawyer and the idea of violating a dead woman were connected in Baudelaire's mind. At this point murder, lust, tenderness and laughter merge (he wanted to show the worker violating his wife's corpse on the stage).

'To see tragic natures founder,' wrote Nietzsche,[24] 'and *to be able to laugh about it* despite the profound understanding, emotion and sympathy one may feel for them, is truly divine.' So inhuman a feeling may well be inaccessible. In order to accede to it, Baudelaire resorted to the feeble device of his hero's decline and the coarseness of his language. But nothing can touch the *peak* that Baudelaire reached with the *Siren*. We can see this from *Les Fleurs du Mal*, which he surpassed in this case. *Les Fleurs du Mal* ensured him a fullness of meaning and he pointed out their accomplishment. Baudelaire never completed his plan to write this play. His laziness or his impotence may have been the reasons. Or did the theatre manager to whom he suggested it inform him of the public's probable reactions? At least, in this outline, Baudelaire went as far as he could. From *Les Fleurs du Mal* to madness it was not the impossible statue but the statue of the impossible of which he dreamed.

THE HISTORICAL SIGNIFICANCE OF *LES FLEURS DU MAL*

The sense – or the non-sense – of Baudelaire's life, the perseverance of that instinct which led him from the poetry of unsatisfaction to the absence contained in total collapse, are not outlined solely in a song. A consistent and *determined* failure, which Sartre attributes to an erroneous choice, proves Baudelaire's horror at the idea of satisfaction. It proves his rejection of the constraints required by material profit. Baudelaire's position was as definite as it could be. In a letter to his mother[25] he expressed a refusal to submit himself to the law of his own will. He wrote:

Finally, it has been *proved* to me this week that I really can earn money – with a little application and perseverance I can earn a great deal of money. But past misfortunes, incessant unhappiness, new debts to pay, the diminution of energy on account of minor annoyances, and finally my tendency to dream have put an end to everything.

We can regard this as an individual characteristic and, as such, as a form of impotence. We can also imagine things in time. We can judge that disgust with work so obviously connected with poetry as if it were an event which corresponded to an objective requirement. We know that Baudelaire submitted himself to this rejection, this aversion, after a deliberate decision and that even Baudelaire had, on various occasions, committed himself unremittingly to the principle of work. 'At every moment,' he wrote in his *Journaux Intimes*,[26] 'we are crushed by the idea and the sensation of time. There are only two ways of escaping from this nightmare, of forgetting it: pleasure and work. Pleasure exhausts us. Work strengthens us. Let us choose.' This attitude was similar to another, expressed a little earlier.[27] 'In every man, at every time, there are two simultaneous tendencies – one towards God, the other towards Satan. The invocation of God or spirituality is a desire to be promoted; that of Satan, or animality, is the joy of descending.'

It is Baudelaire's first statement, however, which has the clearest consequences. Pleasure is the positive form of tangible life: we cannot experience it without an unproductive expenditure of our resources (it exhausts us). Work, on the other hand, is a form of activity. Its effect is the increase of our resources (it strengthens us). Now, 'in every man, at every time, there are two simultaneous tendencies', one towards work (the increase of our resources), the other towards pleasure (the expenditure of our resources). Work corresponds to the care of tomorrow, pleasure to that of the present moment. Work is useful and satisfactory, pleasure useless, leaving a feeling of unsatisfaction. These considerations put economy at the basis of morality and at the basis of poetry. Always, at all times, the choice brings us to the vulgar and materialistic question: 'Should I expend or increase my present resources?'

Baudelaire's reply was curious. On the one hand his notes are filled with the determination to work, but on the other, his life was a long rejection of productive activity. He even wrote: 'To be a useful man has always seemed to me ghastly'. The same impossible resolution of this opposition in favour of Good can be found on other levels. Not only did he choose God, as he chose work, in a completely nominal way, in order to belong to Satan more intimately, but he could not even decide whether the opposition was his own, within himself (between pleasure and work) or external (between God and the devil). All we can say is that he was inclined to reject its transcendental form. What in fact won the day with him was the refusal to work, to be satisfied by it. He only maintained the transcendence of obligation in order to accentuate the value of a rejection and to experience more forcefully the agonising attraction of an unsatisfactory life.

But this was not an individual error. The weakness of Sartre's analysis is exactly that he is content with this aspect. This is what reduces it to negative observations which have only to be situated in time or history for us to get a positive view. The collective relationship between production and expenditure is in history – Baudelaire's experience is in history. Positively, it has that precise sense which history confers upon it.

Like every activity, poetry can be regarded from an economic point of view. So can morality. Indeed, because of his life, and his unhappy reflections, Baudelaire placed the crucial problem in this domain. Sartre both broaches and avoids this question. He has made the mistake of representing poetry and the poet's moral attitude as the result of a choice. If we admit that the individual has made a choice, the sense of what he created is to be found, by others, in the needs which he has satisfied. The true sense of a poem by Baudelaire is not contained in his errors but in the historically determined expectation to which these errors corresponded. According to Sartre, choices similar to those made by Baudelaire appear to have been possible at other times. But they have never, before or since, had as their consequence poems similar to *Les Fleurs du Mal*. Sartre's critique does indeed contain some profound insights, although it neglects this fact. But it cannot account for the fullness with which Baudelaire's poetry has invaded the modern mind. Or, we might say, it only accounts for it inversely, inverted detraction turning unexpectedly to comprehension. Apart from an element of grace, or of luck, Baudelaire's 'unparalleled tension' not only expressed individual necessity: it was also the result of a *material* tension imposed, historically, from without.

In as far as it surpassed the individual instant, the society in which the poet wrote *Les Fleurs du Mal* corresponded to two simultaneous tendencies which are for ever demanding a decision: society, like the individual, is forced to choose between care of the future and that of the present moment. Society is essentially based on the weakness of the individuals for which its own strength compensates. In a sense it is that which the individual is not – it is bound to the primacy of the future. Yet it cannot deny the present; that remains an element about which no definite decision is reached. This is where festivity comes in.[28] During feasts, sacrifice constitutes the significant moment: it concentrates the attention on the expenditure of resources for the sake of the present moment – the expenditure of those very resources which care for the morrow should warn us to preserve.

But the society in which *Les Fleurs du Mal* was written

was no longer that ambiguous society which sustained the primacy of the future and left the nominal presence of the present in a sacred form (disguised as a value of the future, a transcendental, eternal object, an immutable foundation of Good). It was capitalist society in full swing. It reserved as many of the products of work as possible for the increase of the means of production. This society was prepared to crush the luxury of the great even by terror. It turned away from a caste which had exploited the ambiguity of ancient society to its own advantage. It could not forgive it for having used for personal glory a part of the resources (of work) which could have been employed for the increase of the means of production.

Yet between the great lakes of Versailles and the dams of the industrial age, a decision was taken which was not merely in favour of the community opposed to privilege. The decision opposed the increase of productive forces for unproductive pleasure. In the middle of the nineteenth century, bourgeois society chose the dams: it introduced a radical alteration into the world. Between the day of Charles Baudelaire's birth and the moment of his death, Europe was covered by a network of railways. Production opened the prospect of an indefinite increase of productive forces and adopted that increase as its goal. The process which had been prepared some time earlier started a swift metamorphosis of the civilised world based on the primacy of the future – capitalist accumulation.

The proletariat had to oppose this process in so far as it was limited to the increase of the capitalists' personal profit: hence the workers' movements. The same process provoked the romantic protest among writers because it put an end to the splendour of the *ancien régime* and replaced glory by utility. These two protests, therefore, though different in nature, were directed against the same object. The workers' movement, which was not opposed to the principle of accumulation, offered the liberation of man from the slavery of work as its goal. Romanticism, on the other hand, gave a concrete form to the prevention of man's reduction to utilitarian values. Traditional literature simply expressed the non-utilitarian values (military, religious, erotic) admitted by society or the ruling class, while romanticism expressed the values denied by the modern State and bourgeois activity. But although it assumed a precise form, this type of expression was no less dubious. Romanticism was often limited to the exaltation of the past in an ingenuous opposition to the present. It was little more than a compromise: the values of the past had themselves come to terms with utilitarian principles. The theme of nature, which might seem to constitute a more radical form of opposition, merely offered the possibility of a provisional escape. Besides, love of nature can so easily be conciliated with the primacy of utility, that is to say of the future, that it has been the most common – and the most harmless – means of compensating for utilitarian societies. There is obviously nothing less dangerous, less subversive, or even less wild than the wildness of rocks.

At first sight the romantic position of the *individual* is of greater consequence. To start with, the individual opposes social constraint by a dreamy, passionate existence which rebels against discipline. Yet the demands of the living individual are far from being consistent. They lack the hard and lasting coherence of a religious morality or of the code of honour of a certain caste. The only constant element among individuals is interest in increasing resources which the capitalist enterprises have the opportunity of satisfying. The individual is therefore the goal of bourgeois society just as hierarchy is the goal of feudal society.

Let us add that the pursuit of private interest is both the source and the end of capitalist activity. The great poetic form of individualism may seem excessive as a response, but nevertheless it is a response to utilitarian calculation. In its sacred form romanticism was no more than an antibourgeois aspect of bourgeois individualism. Anguish, self-denial, nostalgia for the unobtainable expressed the unease of the bourgeoisie who, once they had entered history by committing themselves to the refusal of responsibility, expressed the opposite to what they were, but made sure that they never suffered the consequences of this opposite or benefited from them in any way. In literature, denial of the basis of capitalist activity only escaped belatedly from compromise. It was only at the peak of their activity and their development, after the sharp attack of romantic fever, that the bourgeoisie felt at ease.

At this point literary research was no longer limited by a possibility of compromise. Baudelaire, it is true, had nothing radical about him – he always retained the desire not to have the impossible as his lot and to return to favour. But, as Sartre helps us to realise, he drew from his failure what others drew from rebellion. He had no will power, but an instinct animated him in spite of himself. Charles Baudelaire's refusal was the most profound form of refusal, for it was in no way the assertion of an opposite principle. It only expressed that which was indefensible and impossible in the poet's obstructed state of mind.

Evil, which the poet does not so much perpetrate as he experiences its fascination, is indeed Evil since the will, which can only desire Good, has no part in it. Besides, it hardly matters whether it is Evil. If the contrary of will is fascination, if fascination is the destruction of the will, to condemn behaviour regulated by fascination on moral grounds may be the only way of really liberating it from the will. Religion, castes, and, more recently, romanticism, had been a means of seduction. But then these very means of seduction began to use trickery, and obtained the approval of a will which was also prepared to use trickery. Poetry, therefore, which hoped to seduce the senses, had to limit its objects of seduction to those regulated by the will (conscious will which insists on such conditions as survival and satisfaction). Ancient poetry limited the liberty implicated in poetry. In the turgid mass of these waters Baudelaire opened a trough of cursed poetry which no longer assumed anything and which submitted itself to a fascination incapable of giving satisfaction, a fascination which was purely destructive. Thus poetry turned away from extrinsic requirements, from the requirements of the will, in order to satisfy one single intimate requirement which connected it with that which fascinated, which made it the opposite of will.

There is something other than the choice of a weak individual in this major determination of poetry. It hardly matters whether a personal inclination, involving responsibility, sheds any light on the circumstances of the poet's life. For us the significance of *Les Fleurs du Mal*, and therefore of Baudelaire, results from our intererst in poetry. We would care nothing about an individual destiny were it not for the interest aroused by the poems. So we can only discuss it to the extent in which it is illustrated by our love for *Les Fleurs du Mal* – that is to say, not separately, but in connection with the whole. The poet's curious attitude towards morality accounts for the break which he effected: in Baudelaire the denial of Good was basically a denial of the primacy of the future. At the same time the assertion of Good contained an element of maturity (which regulated his attitude towards eroticism). It revealed to him both regularly and unfortunately (in a cursed way) the paradox of the instant to which we can only accede by fleeing from it and which eludes us if we try to seize it. There is no doubt that we can rise above Baudelaire's humiliating – and accursed – attitude, but even if we do so we cannot come to rest. We find the same humiliating misfortune in other, less passive, more reduced forms, which leave no subterfuge. So hard, or so extravagant, are they, that one might almost say that they constitute a savage happiness.

Baudelaire's poetry itself has been surpassed. The contradiction between a rejection of Good (of a value imposed by the will for survival) and the creation of a work which will survive, places poetry on that path of rapid decomposition where it was conceived, increasingly negatively, as a perfect silence of the will.

NOTES

1. J.-P. Sartre, *Baudelaire*. Gallimard, 1946. This essay on Baudelaire was written on the publication of Sartre's book.
2. J.-P. Sartre, Ibid.
3. Ibid.
4. Ibid.
5. Ibid.
6. Ibid.
7. Ibid.
8. Ibid.
9. Ibid.
10. Ibid. And further on.
11. Ibid.
12. Here is the full sentence:

    'It is this determination of the present by the future, of what exists by what does not yet exist, that he (Baudelaire) called "unsatisfaction" – and we shall return to this later – and which philosophers today call transcendence.' He continues, on page 204, 'Significance, the image of human transcendence, is like the object surpassing itself... An intermediary between the present thing which supports it and the absent object which it designates, it keeps in itself a little of the former and already heralds the latter. For Baudelaire it was the very symbol of unsatisfaction.'

13. Op. cit.
14. Ibid.
15. Sartre's italics.
16. Op. cit.
17. My italics.
18. Op. cit.
19. In the sense of that which is not subordinated to anything other than its primary impulse and which is indifferent to every external consideration.

20. In the sense of that which is not subordinated to anything other than its primary impulse and which is indifferent to every external consideration.
21. Op. cit.
22. *Correspondance générale*. Recueillie, classée et annotée par J. Crêpet, Conard.
23. In *Les Fleurs du Mal*, *Le Vin de l'assassin*, a poem about a sawyer, is one of the most mediocre in the whole collection. The character is imprisoned by Baudelaire's rhythm. What we glimpsed in an outline outside the poetic formula falls back into the furrow.
24. *Nachlass, 1882–1884*.
25. *Correspondance générale*. The letter is dated March 26, 1853.
26. *Mon coeur mis à nu*, LXXXIX.
27. Ibid. XIX.
28. The 'cursed share' which I mentioned in the previous chapter. See supra p. 17.

MICHELET

Few men have staked everything as candidly as Michelet on a few simple ideas. He believed the progress of Truth and Justice, and a return to the laws of Nature, to be inevitable. In this sense his work is a magnificent act of faith. But though he never really perceived the limitations of reason, he occasionally (I dwell on the paradox) came to the assistance of those very passions which opposed it. I do not know how he came to write a book like *La Sorcière* – by chance, no doubt: his decision was apparently due to certain files, hitherto unused and compiled over the years, which he was determined to edit. In any case, *La Sorcière* makes its author appear as one of the men who have spoken most humanely about Evil.

It seems to me that he went astray. Yet the roads which he took – at random and guided by an 'unhealthy' curiosity – lead towards our truths. They are the roads of Evil: not of the Evil which we do by abusing strength at the expense of the weak, but of the Evil which goes against our own interests and which is brought about by a passionate desire for liberty. Michelet saw it as a deviation taken by Good. He tried to justify it: the witch was the victim who died in the horror of the flames. It was natural to reverse the values of the theologians. Was not Evil on the side of the executioner? The witch was the incarnation of suffering humanity, persecuted by the strong. Though these views were no doubt partially correct, they ran the immediate risk of preventing the historian from seeing any further. Michelet was guided by the ecstasy of Evil: he was bewildered by it.

The abyss of Evil is attractive independently of the profit to be gained by wicked actions – or at least by some of them. But if we imagine the paths of Evil in their entirety, how very few of them really satisfy our interests. Such an attraction, which springs most obviously from the horror of the sabbaths, can serve to define the difficulty of the moral problem in all its depth. *La Sorcière* is one of the more reputable books on magic in Christian society. None of them satisfy the requisites of science, but *La Sorcière* is Michelet's masterpiece, and it gives me the opportunity of setting out the problem of Evil dispassionately.

THE SACRIFICE

The facts of this problem are connected with their historical origins, constituted by the contrast between malefice and sacrifice. Nowhere is this contrast so great as in the Christian world, where we see it by the light of innumerable stakes.[1] But it exists in a similar form at all times and in all places; its constant exists both in social initiative, which constitutes the religious dignity of sacrifice, and in particular, as opposed to social, initiative, which brings us to the least commendable aspect of malefice connected with the practice of magic. Such a constant undoubtedly corresponds to an elementary necessity which should be perfectly obvious.

What we must demonstrate is that, just as certain insects, in given conditions, flock towards a ray of light, so we all flock to an area at the opposite end of the scale from death. The mainspring of human activity is generally the desire to reach the point farthest from the funereal domain, which is rotten, dirty and impure. We make every effort to efface the traces, signs and symbols of death. Then, if we can, we efface the traces and signs of these efforts. Our desire to elevate ourselves is one of a hundred symptoms of this force which guides us to the antipodes of death. The disgust the rich feel for the workers, the panic which seizes hold of the petty bourgeois at the idea of lapsing into the condition of the proletariat, depend on the fact that in their eyes the poor are closer to death than themselves. On occasion it is those shady paths of filth, impotence and destruction which lead towards death that are the objects of our aversion, rather than death itself.

This distressing inclination may play a greater part in our assertion of moral principles than in our reflexes. Our assertions are no doubt veiled. Great words give a positive sense to a negative attitude – a positive sense which is evidently empty but which is adorned with the splendour of brilliant values. All we can propose is the good of all – easy gain and assured peace – legitimate but purely negative aims, which are really ways of banishing death. Our general concepts of life can always be reduced to the desire to survive. This applies as much to Michelet as to the wisest of men.

This attitude and these principles are immutable – or at least in as far as they are, and must remain, a basis. And yet we can only agree up to a point. Even if we limit our research to the interest which men pursue, we will find it necessary to raise an objection. Life sometimes fails to flee from the shades of death. It allows them to grow within it, to the point of exhaustion, to the point of death itself. The constant recurrence of abominated elements, the opposite of those of which the impulses of life are directed, exists to a mitigated extent in normal conditions – to an extent too mitigated for the shades of death to be reborn *in spite of ourselves*. We must still revive them voluntarily – in a way which corresponds precisely to our needs (I refer to the shades, not to death itself). It is to this purpose that we put the arts: they manage, on the stage, to arouse in us the highest possible degree of anxiety. The arts – or at least some of the arts – incessantly evoke these derangements, these lacerations, this decline which our entire activity endeavours to avoid. Indeed, comic art itself confirms this theory.

However little weight the elements which we want to eliminate from our life, but which the arts bring back to us, may have, they are nevertheless the signs of death. If we laugh or if we cry it is because, as victims of a game or depositories of a secret, death momentarily appears light to us. That does not mean that it has lost its horror: it simply means that for an instant we have risen above it. The vital impulses provoked in this way no doubt lack practical consequences: they do not have that convincing power of impulses which stem from aversion and which remind us that work is necessary. Nevertheless they have a value. Laughter teaches us that when we flee wisely from the elements of death, we merely want to *preserve life*. When we enter the regions that wisdom tells us to avoid, on the other hand, we really *live it*. The folly of laughter is superficial. It burns as it comes into contact with death; from the symbols of the emptiness of death it draws a heightened consciousness of being. As it violently introduces something which we should have cast aside, it brings us out, for a time, from the impasse in which life is enclosed by those whose only concern is to preserve it.

I would like to go beyond my limited purpose of presenting the problem of Evil rationally and say that the being which we are is primarily a finite being (a mortal individual). His limitations are no doubt necessary to the being, but he cannot endure them. It is by going beyond these limitations which are necessary for his preservation that he asserts the nature of his being. We must admit that the finite character of the only beings which we know would be contrary to other characteristics of being, were it not alleviated by an extreme instability. No matter: all I must do is recall that those arts which sustain anguish and the recovery from anguish within us are the heirs of religion. Our tragedies and our comedies are the continuation of ancient sacrificial rites. Almost every people attributed the greatest importance to the ritual destruction of animals, men or vegetables. Some were immensely valuable, others were merely supposed to be valuable. Initially these acts of destruction were considered criminal, but the community was obliged to perform them.

Since sacrifices were said to serve so many purposes, we must seek the origins of so widespread a practice further back. The most discerning individuals saw sacrifice as an institution on which the social bond was based, though no reason was ever given why the spilling of blood, rather than some other means, lay at the foundation of the social bond. But if we must approach as closely as possible, and as often as possible, the very object of our disgust, if our nature can be defined by *introducing into life the greatest number of elements which contradict it, but at the same time harm it as little as possible*, sacrifice no longer remains that elementary, but none the less intelligible, form of behaviour which it has been hitherto. So eminent a custom had, in the end, 'to correspond to some elementary necessity which should be perfectly obvious'.

The 'greatest number' was, of course, usually small, and people resorted to many a trick in order to minimise the danger. This depended on relative strength: if any nation had the courage, it pushed things farther. The Aztec hecatombs reveal the degree of horror which a people could reach. The thousands of Aztec victims of Evil were not only captives: the altars were fed by wars, and death in battle expressly associated the tribesmen with the ritual death of the victims. At certain feasts the Mexicans even sacrificed their own children. This gives an unpleasantly clear idea of a process which was to reach an almost intolerable pitch of horror. A law had to be established which ordained the punishment of men who turned away from the procession as the children were led to the temple. The extreme limit of such a ceremony was unconsciousness.

If human life did not contain this violent instinct, we could dispense with the arts. The fact that moments of intensity are necessary for the foundation of the social bond is of secondary interest. There is no doubt that the bond has to have some foundation, and we can easily see how this came to be sacrifice. For the moments of intensity are the moments of excess and of fusion of beings. But human beings were not brought to a point of fusion because they had to form societies, as we might melt various pieces of metal in order to make one new one. When we reach states of fusion (laughter and tears are cases in point) through anguish and the transcendence of anguish, it seems to me that, with the means peculiar to men, we satisfy an elementary requirement of finite beings.

MALEFICE AND THE BLACK MASS

The institution of the social bond, far from being the origin of sacrifice, is such that it might almost diminish its power. In the city sacrifice was performed in a high place. It was connected with the purest, holiest and, at the same time, the most conservative cares – like the maintenance of life and work. In fact, what it intends to set up has relatively little do do with the initial instinct behind it. The same does not apply to malefice. The authors of sacrifice were aware of the crime they were committing, but they performed it for the greater good. Good was always the ultimate end of sacrifice, so the whole process was really mutilated: it was almost a failure. Malefice does not, of course, originate in the failure of sacrifice and it does not fail for the same reasons. It was carried out for alien ends, often opposed to Good – for this, and for no other essential reason, it differs from sacrifice. In these circumstances the transgression on which it was based was not going to diminish: it was, in all probability, going to be accentuated.

Sacrifice would seem to reduce the intrusion of troubled elements. It rests on the contradiction made evident by emphasising the purity and the nobility of the victims and the places. Malefice, on the other hand, can insist on a heavy, negative element. Though it is not essential to magic, it uses magic as its domain. In the Middle Ages witchcraft became the very opposite of religion which merged with morality. We know little about the sabbath. We only know about the repressive process and that the exhausted defendants made confessions forced upon them by their inquisitors, but we cannot agree with Michelet that what we call the Black Mass was the parody of Christian sacrifice. Even if the traditional accounts were to some extent imaginary, they did have certain things in common with the true facts: they had the significative value of a myth or a dream.

The human mind, submitted to Christian morality, tends to develop contradictions which have suddenly become possible. We can consider any road valid if it helps us to come closer to the object of our disgust. Basing himself on an ecclesiastical report, Michelet evoked the mental instinct which advances, hesitates, but is fatally drawn to the worst. 'Some,' he wrote, 'only saw terror; others were moved by the melancholy pride in which the eternal Exile seemed absorbed.' This god, whose 'back' the faithful 'preferred', who made no attempt to ensure the public welfare, corresponded to a resolute step towards darkness. The image of God's humiliating death, the most paradoxical and the richest of images, was surpassed by this inversion. The particular situation of magic, unlimited by a feeling of responsibility or degree, conferred on the black mass the sense of an extreme possibility.

The unrecognised greatness of this ritual defilement which symbolised a nostalgia for infinite defilement, cannot be overrated. It is like a parasite: it is the inversion of the Christian theme. But inversion, springing from an excessive audacity, is the culmination of an instinct to regain that which our desire to survive forces us to avoid. At the end of the Middle Ages the popular development of the sabbaths may have corresponded to the decline of the Church – it was, in a way, its dying light. The countless stakes, every kind of torture devised by the priests, suggest this. The exceptional quality of the moment is also emphasised by the fact that nations subsequently lost the power to requite their dreams by way of ritual. Thus the sabbath may be considered a last word. The mythical man is dead, leaving us this final message – a black laugh.

It is to Michelet's credit to have accorded these nonsensical feasts the value due to them. He gave them a human warmth which is less that of the body than of the heart. We cannot be sure whether he was right to connect the sabbaths with those 'great and terrible revolts', the peasant revolts of the Middle Ages. But the ritual of witchcraft is the ritual of an oppressed people. The religion of a conquered nation has often become the magic of societies formed as a result of the conquest. The mediaeval rites were undoubtedly a continuation of the religion of the ancients, though there is a certain confusion as to the identification of the deities: in a sense Satan was a *Dionysos redivivus*. They were the rites of the *pagani*, of peasants and serfs, victims of a dominant order, and a dominant religion. Nothing concerning this lower world is clear, but Michelet must nevertheless be given credit for having spoken of it as of our world, animated by our own hearts, carrying with it the hope and despair which are our lot and in which we recognise ourselves.

Michelet's assertion of the eminence of women in these accursed activities is fully acceptable. This realm of darkness is illuminated by caprice and female gentleness. At the same time something of the witch is bound up with the idea we may have of seduction. The exaltation of women and love, which is today at the basis of our moral wealth, does not only originate from the legends of chivalry but from women's role in magic. 'For one warlock, ten thousand witches...' Torture, the tongs and the flames awaited them.

That Michelet should have extracted this very human world from shame is admirable. The first edition of *La Sorcière* caused a scandal under Napoleon and the police withdrew it from the bookshops. The book was published in Brussels by Lacroix and Verboeckhoven (who published that epic of Evil, *Les Chants de Maldoror*, a few years later). Michelet's weakness – but is this not the weakness of human intelligence? – is to have made the witch the servant of Good in his fervent desire to rescue her from opprobrium. He wanted to justify her by attributing to her a form of *utility*, which her true activity would seem to deny.

GOOD, EVIL, 'VALUE' AND MICHELET'S LIFE

I shall now conclude this account of the problem of Evil. Certain facts should emerge from the picture I have given. Humanity pursues two goals – one, the negative, is to preserve life (to avoid death), and the other, the positive, is to increase the intensity of life. These two goals are not contradictory, but their intensity has never increased without danger. The intensity desired by the greater number (or the social body) is subordinated to the care of preserving life and its works - a care which takes unquestioned precedence. But when minorities or individuals try to acquire this intensity, they can strive in vain, beyond their desire to survive. The intensity varies according to the greater or the lesser liberty. The opposition between intensity and survival is valid. We see it in religious asceticism and, where magic is concerned, in the pursuit of individual ends.[2] Good and Evil must, therefore, be reconsidered in this light.

Intensity can be defined as a value (it is the only positive value), survival as Good (it is the general goal of virtue). The notion of intensity cannot be reduced to that of pleasure because, as we have seen, the quest for intensity leads us into the realm of unease and then to the limits of consciousness. So what I call value differs where Good and pleasure are concerned. Sometimes the value coincides with Good, sometimes it does not. It sometimes coincides with Evil. The value is situated *beyond Good and Evil*, but in two opposed forms, one connected with the principle of Good, the other with that of Evil. The desire for Good limits the instinct which induces us to seek a value, whereas liberty towards Evil gives access to the excessive forms of value. Yet we cannot conclude from this that authentic value is on the side of Evil. The very principle of value wants us to go 'as far as possible'. In this respect the association with the principle of Good establishes the 'farthest point' from the social body, beyond which constituted society cannot advance, while the association with the principle of Evil establishes the 'farthest point' which individuals or minorities can temporarily reach. Nobody can go any 'farther'.

There is also a third case. Some minority may, at one

moment in its history, rise above the pure and simple revolt and gradually assume the obligations of a social body. The possibilities of this last case remain fluid.

I must here point out that Michelet never solved the problem. He attributed to the world he represented more than a mere desire to rebel. He attributed to it a more elevated concern with ensuring the future, with survival, and he thereby imposed severe limitations on it. Let this be said without disparaging him – I would really like to convey a feeling of power – Michelet's life itself corresponded to this ambivalence. He was obviously dominated, and even bewildered, by anxiety as he wrote this impassioned book. In a passage from his diary (I have been unable to read it since it is still inaccessible, but a third party has provided me with adequate information), he said that as he worked he would suddenly find that he lacked inspiration. He then would leave his house and go to a public convenience where the stink was stultifying. He would breathe in deeply and then, having 'got as close as possible to the object of his disgust', return to work. I cannot but recall his face – noble, emaciated, with quivering nostrils.

NOTES

1. We know little about witchcraft itself. What we know is mainly taken from the proceedings of the trials and it is to be feared that the inquisitors used torture in order to force their victims to say what they wanted them to say, not what really happened. Nevertheless we know some precise facts concerning the repression directed against witchcraft, all of which were familiar to Michelet.
2. These ends usually tend towards excess, not towards pure and simple Good or conservation. They therefore lend themselves to intensity.

WILLIAM BLAKE

If I had to name those English writers who moved me most, they would be John Ford, Emily Brontë and William Blake.[1] I agree that such classifications are pretty meaningless, yet these names have certain powers in common. They have just emerged from obscurity and in the excessive violence of their work, Evil attains a form of purity.

Ford left an incomparable image of criminal love. Emily Brontë saw the wickedness of a foundling as the only clear answer to the demands which consumed her. Blake managed, in phrases of a peremptory simplicity, to reduce humanity to poetry and poetry to Evil.

WILLIAM BLAKE'S LIFE AND WORK

William Blake's life seems almost banal: it was regular and unadventurous. And yet it had one striking peculiarity: it escaped, to a large extent, from the common limitations of life. His contemporaries were not unaware of his existence. In his lifetime he enjoyed a certain notoriety, but he was always alone - he never formed part of a group. If Wordsworth and Coleridge appreciated him, it was not without reservations. Coleridge, at least, complained of the indecency of his writings. He had, on the whole, to be set aside, to be kept in the background. 'He is a lunatic,' they said of him, and continued to repeat it even after his death.[2] His works (his writings and his paintings) have a maladjusted quality. They astonish us with their indifference to common rules. Something exorbitant, deaf to the reproaches of others, raises these poems and these violently coloured figures to a sublime level. Though Blake was a visionary he never gave a real value to his visions. He was not mad: he simply saw them as human, the creations of the human mind.

It has been stated, a little oddly,[3] that

> many others... have descended into the unconscious as far as Blake, but they have not returned. The asylums are full of them; for the modern definition of a madman is one who has been overwhelmed by the symbols of the unconscious. Blake is the only one who has ventured as far as they and yet remained sane. Pure poets, who had no other lifeline connected with the world above than their own poetry, have succumbed – Nietzsche, Hölderlin.

This interpretation of reason may be reasonable in that poetry appears contrary to reason. If a poet's life conformed generally to reason it would go against the irreducible element, a sovereign violence from poetry, without which it is mutilated. The true poet is like a child in the world. He may, like Blake or like a child, be gifted with an unquestionable common sense, but he cannot be entrusted with the management of business. The poet is eternally under-age: hence the laceration of which Blake's life and work are made. Blake, who was not mad, haunted the frontiers of madness.

Throughout his life the visions of his poetic genius had precedence over the prosaic reality of the outer world. This is particularly curious in that he was, and never ceased to be, a member of the poorer classes – one for whom such a choice is especially difficult. For the rich man this choice may be an affectation which would not survive the loss of his wealth. The poor man, on the other hand, is tempted to concentrate his energies on complaining about his lot.

William Blake was born in London in 1757, the son of a poor hatter (of Irish origin, no doubt). He only had a rudimentary education, but he owed it to his father's solicitude and to his own exceptional talents – he wrote remarkable poems when he was twelve and showed a rare gift for drawing – that he entered an engraver's workshop at the age of fourteen. He had difficulty in earning his living and disconcerted his buyers by his fantastic compositions. He was constantly encouraged by the love of his wife, Catherine Bouchez, a woman who had the elongated stature of his female figures, who could calm him during his attacks of fever and who nursed him for forty-five years until his death in 1827. He felt that he had a supernatural mission and his dignity never failed to impress those around him. But his political and moral ideas were considered scandalous. He wore a red hat when Londoners saw the French Jacobins as their most dreaded enemies. He wrote an apology for sexual freedom and, rumour had it, wanted to force his wife to live with his mistress.

In fact his life was an inner phenomenon and the mythical figures which populated Blake's private world were the negation of external reality, moral laws and all that they entailed. In his eyes the fragile figure of Catherine Bouchez assumed a significance in so far as it merged with the angels of his visions. Yet it seems likely that he sometimes denied the conventional principles which limited her outlook. Even his friends, like the historical events of his time, had to become part of a transfiguration where they joined the divine personages of the past. A poem contained in a letter to the sculptor John Flaxman, dated 12 September, 1800, gives an account of this transposition from the external to the internal:

When Flaxman was taken to Italy, Fuseli was given to
me for a season,
And now Flaxman hath given me Hayley his friend to
be mine, such my lot upon Earth.
Now my lot in the Heavens is this, Milton lov'd me in
childhood and shew'd me his face.
Ezra came with Isaiah the Prophet, but Shakespeare
in riper years gave me his hand...
And in Hell beneath, & a mighty & awful change
threatened the Earth.
The American War began. All its dark horrors passed
before my face.
Across the Atlantic to France. Then the French
Revolution commenc'd in thick clouds,
And my Angels have told me that seeing such visions
I could not subsist on the Earth,
But by my conjunction with Flaxman, who knows to
forgive Nervous Fear.[4]

THE SOVEREIGNTY OF POETRY

An attempt has been made to interpret William Blake's 'psychology' (or mythology) by introducing it into C. G. Jung's category of 'introversion'. According to Jung, 'introverted intuition perceives all the background processes of consciousness with almost the same distinctness as extraverted sensation senses outer objects. For intuition, therefore, the unconscious images attain to the dignity of things, or objects.'[5] W. P. Witcutt is right to quote, in this context, Blake's statement that 'Man's perceptions are not bounded by organs of perception; he perceives more than sense (tho' ever so acute) can discover.'[6] But Jung's vocabulary contains an element of fluidity: the perception which cannot be reduced to the sense-data does not only inform us of that which is within us (of that which is introverted in us). It is poetic feeling. Though poetry does not accept sense-data in their naked state, it is by no means always contemptuous of the outer world. Rather, it challenges the precise limitations of objects between themselves, while admitting their external nature. It denies and it destroys immediate reality because it sees in it the screen which conceals the true face of the world from us. Nevertheless poetry admits the exteriority of tools or of walls *in relation to the ego*. Blake's lesson is founded on the value in itself, extrinsic to the ego, of poetry. We read in a significant passage:[7]

> The Poetic Genius is the true Man, and ... the body or outward form of Man is derived from the Poetic Genius ... As all men are alike in outward form, so (and with the same infinite variety) all are alike in the Poetic Genius ... The Religions of all Nations are derived from each Nation's different reception of the Poetic Genius ... As all men are alike (tho' infinitely various), So all Religions &, as all similars, have one source. The true Man is the source, he being the Poetic Genius.

This identification of man and poetry not only has the power to distinguish between morals and religion, and to turn religions into the work of man (not of God or of the transcendency of reason), but it also returns to poetry the world in which we move. This world cannot be reduced to the things which are both alien to us and enslaved by us. It is not the profane, prosaic, unseductive world of work – only in the eyes of 'introverts' who see no poetry in exteriority can the truth of the world be reduced to that of the thing. Poetry alone, which denies and destroys the limitations of things, can return us to this absence of limitations – in short, the world is given to us when the image which we have within us is sacred, because all that is sacred is poetic and all that is poetic is sacred.

For religion is nothing but the effect of poetic genius. There is nothing in religion which cannot be found in poetry. There is nothing which does not bind the poet to humanity and humanity to the universe. Usually a formal, fixed element, subordinate to the needs of a group (and therefore to the utilitarian and profane needs[8] of morality) moves religion away from poetic truth. Similarly, poetry is formally abandoned to the impotence of servile beings. We encounter the same difficulty at each step: each general truth looks like a particular lie. There is not a religion or a poem which does not lie. There is not a religion or a poem which cannot sometimes be reduced to public lack of recognition from outside. Nevertheless religion and poetry never fail to propel us outside ourselves in great bursts in which death is no longer the opposite of life. The very poverty of poetry or religion depends on the extent to which the introvert reduces them to obsession with his personal feelings. Blake's achievement was to strip the individual figure of both poetry and religion and to return to them that clarity in which religion has the liberty of poetry and poetry the sovereign power of religion.

BLAKE'S MYTHOLOGY INTERPRETED IN THE LIGHT OF JUNG'S PSYCHOANALYSIS

No true introversion of Blake's had only one sense. His introversions involved particularity and the arbitrary choice of those myths which he elaborated. What, for anyone other than Blake, is the meaning of the divine figures of his universe who go in for interminable battles in endless poems?

Blake's mythology generally introduced the problem of poetry. When poetry expresses the myths which tradition proposes to it, it is not autonomous: it does not contain sovereignty within itself. It humbly illustrates the legend whose form and meaning can exist without it. If it is the autonomous work of a visionary, it defines furtive apparitions which do not have the power to convince and only have a real significance for the poet. Thus autonomous poetry, even if it only appears to be the creation of a myth, is a mere absence of myth. Indeed, this world in which we live no longer engenders new myths, and the myths which poetry seems to establish only really reveal the void, unless they are objects of faith. To talk of Enitharmon is not to reveal the truth about Enitharmon. One might almost say that it is to admit the absence of Enitharmon in a world to which poetry summons him in vain. The paradox of Blake is to have returned the essentials of religion to those of poetry and to have at the same time revealed, through lack of strength, that poetry in itself cannot both be free and have a sovereign value. It is to say that it cannot really be both poetry and religion. What it shows is the absence of the religion which it should have been. It is religion in the same way as the memory of a beloved being brings home to us how impossible absence is. It is undoubtedly sovereign, but it is sovereign in the desire for the object, not the possession of it. Poetry is right to assert the extent of its empire, but we cannot contemplate this extent without immediately knowing that it is completely elusive: it is not the empire so much as the impotence of poetry.

At the origin of poetry bonds are shed, and only impotent liberty remains. Milton, Blake once said, 'was a true Poet, and of the Devil's party without knowing it'.

Religion which has the purity of poetry, religion which makes the same demands as poetry, cannot have a greater power than the devil, who is the pure essence of poetry. Even if it wanted to, poetry could not construct: it destroys; it is only true when in revolt. Sin and damnation inspired Milton, while paradise removed his poetic vigour. Similarly, Blake's poetry wasted away far from the 'impossible'. His vast poems, where non-existent phantoms writhe, do not furnish the mind. They empty it and deceive it.

They deceive it, and they are there to deceive it, since they consist of the negation of its common requirements. In the creative moment, Blake's visions were sovereign: the whims of immoderate imagination refused to comply with self-interest. It is not that Urizen and Luvah have no meaning. Luvah is the divinity of passion, Urizen of reason. But these mythical figures do not draw their existence from a logical development of their significance, so it is fruitless to follow them too closely. A methodical study of these figures may reveal details about 'Blake's psychology, but it also makes us lose sight of its most striking characteristic. The violent impulse which animates it cannot be reduced to the expression of logical entities. It is whim itself and the logic of entities is indifferent to it. There is no point in reducing Blake's inventiveness to intelligible propositions or to common measures. W. P. Witcutt wrote that 'Blake's Four Zoas are not . . . peculiar to himself. They form a theme running through all literature, though only Blake presents them as it were in the crude mythological state.'

It is true that Blake himself gave a meaning to three of these dream creatures: Urizen, a formal combination of 'horizon' and 'reason', is the Prince of Light: he is 'God, the terrible destroyer and not the Saviour'. Luvah, whose name evokes the word *love*, is, like the Greek Eros, a child of fire, the living expression of passion:

His nostrils breathe a fiery flame, His locks are like the
forest
Of wild beasts; there the lion glares, the tyger and wolf
howl there,
And there the Eagle hides her young in cliffs and
precipices.
His bosom is like starry heaven expanded...

Los, the 'Spirit of Prophecy' is to Luvah what Dionysos is
to Apollo and he expresses clearly enough the power of the
imagination. Only the meaning of the fourth, Tharmas, is
not explicitly given, but W. P. Witcutt does not hesitate to
interpret it as the fourth function, feeling, thereby
completing the other three functions – thought, intuition
and sensation. Indeed Blake calls the Four Zoas the 'four
eternal Senses of Man'. In each one of us he sees 'Four
Mighty Ones'.

W. P. Witcutt's interpretations are essentially Jungian:
they are, he claims, fundamental, and we find them not
only in the thought of St. Augustine, but in the mythology
of the Egyptians and 'Dumas's *Three Musketeers* – four with
D'Artagnan – (as well as in) Edgar Wallace's *Four Just
Men*'! This type of commentary is less idiotic than it might
seem, but it is precisely because it is reasoned – even
rational – that it remains outside and beyond the shapeless
emotion which Blake wanted to convey. This emotion can
only be grasped in the moment of excess, when it passes the
borders of reason and no longer depends on anything.

William Blake's mythological epic, his sharpness of
vision, his requirements and his profusion, his laceration
and his childishness, his battles between sovereign or rebel
divinities seem the most obvious object for psychoanalysis.
It is easy to perceive the authority of the father and the
revolt of the son. It is natural to search in this relationship
for an attempt to conciliate opposites, the desire for

appeasement lending an ultimate significance to the disorder of war. But what can we find in psychoanalysis, whether it be that of Freud or that of Jung, other than the data of psychoanalysis itself? Thus the attempt to elucidate Blake through Jung tells us more about Jung's theories than about Blake's intentions. It would be fruitless to embark on a detailed discussion of the explanations given, but we can suggest a general thesis. The problem at hand, in the great symbolic poems, is the struggle of divinities incarnating the functions of the soul and, after the struggle, the moment when each lacerated divinity will find his true and predestined place in the hierarchy of the functions. But such a truth, with so vague a meaning, arouses our mistrust. It seems to me that analysis is merely cancelling out a remarkable work and that it is substituting a somnolent heaviness for awakenness. The real answer is the harmony which Blake arrives at in a lacerated condition, while for Jung or for W. P. Witcutt it is the harmony – the end – of the journey which matters, rather than the agitated journey itself.

This reduction of Blake to Jung's interpretations can be defended, but it is not entirely satisfactory. For when we read Blake we hope that the world will not be reduced to those closed categories in which everything has been played out in advance, in which there is no quest, no agitation, no awakening, in which all we can do is to follow the track, sleep and breathe in time to the universal clock of sleep.

THE LIGHT THROWN ON EVIL: 'THE MARRIAGE OF HEAVEN AND HELL'

The dreamlike incoherence of Blake's visionary writings offers no opposition to the clarity which psychoanalysis would like to introduce. And yet we must emphasise this incoherence. Madeleine L. Cazamian wrote:

> During these exuberant and complicated accounts the same characters die, are resurrected and reborn at various times in different circumstances. At one point Los and Enitharmon are the children of Tharmas and his emanation, Eon, and Urizen is their son; elsewhere he is engendered by Vola. The creation of the world is therefore no longer attributed to him – only its organisation according to the laws of reason. Later, in *Jerusalem*, it will become the work of Elohim, another of the Eternals, or else it will emanate entirely from the 'universal Man'. In the *Four Zoas* Urizen is called Urthona and becomes the ghost of Los; in yet another poem, *Milton*, he is identified with Satan. He is a dark monster from another light; after the North, with its shades and its frosts, other cardinal points are attributed to him according to the symbolic design in which he is incorporated. Now, he was, and usually remains, the Jehovah of the Bible, the jealous creator of the Mosaic religion, the founder of the law. But in *Jerusalem*, Jehovah is invoked as the God of forgiveness, while 'the lamb' or Christ distributes special grace. Elsewhere, when Blake personifies the imaginative vision, he calls it Jehovah-Elohim. It is impossible to attempt a full interpretation. The poet seems to live in a nightmare, or in a daze... [9]

Chaos can be one means of arriving at a definable possibility, but if we look back at the works of Blake's youth chaos must be understood as something *impossible*, as a poetic violence and not as a calculated order. The chaos of the mind cannot constitute a reply to the providence of the universe. All it can be is an *awakening* in the night, where all that can be heard is anguished poetry let loose.

What is so striking in Blake's life and work is its *presence* before everything proposed by the world. We may come close to seeing Blake as the Jungian 'introvert' if we say that there is nothing seductive, simple or happy which he had not prayed for – songs, the laughter of childhood, the games of sensuality, the warmth and the drunkenness of the tavern. Nothing irritated him so much as the moral law which denied enjoyment.

But if at the Church they would give us some Ale,
And a pleasant fire our souls to regale.[10]

This ingenuousness fully exposed the young poet guileless before life. A work loaded with horror began with the gaiety of the 'pipes', when Blake wrote his 'happy songs Every child may joy to hear'. And this joy announced the strangest marriage pipes were ever to announce. With youthful audacity the poet confronted every antimony. The marriage which he wished to celebrate was the marriage of Heaven and Hell.

We must examine Blake's curious words attentively. They are heavy with historical significance. What they describe is ultimately man's compliance with his own laceration, his compliance with death and the instinct which propels him towards it. They go beyond purely poetic words. They are an exact reflection of a definitive return to the totality of human destiny. Blake was subsequently to express his agitation in a lost and disorderly manner, but he was at the *peak* of the disorder which possessed him. From this peak he saw, in its integrity and violence, the extent of the instinct which propels us towards the worst, but at the same time raises us to glory. Blake was in no way a philosopher, but he pronounced the essential with a vigour and a precision that might make a philosopher envious. He wrote:[11]

Without Contraries, is no progression. Attraction and Repulsion, Reason and Energy, Love and Hate, are necessary to Human existence.

From these contraries spring what the religious call Good and Evil. Good is the passive that obeys Reason. Evil is the active springing from Energy.

Good is Heaven. Evil is Hell...

God will torment Man in Eternity for following his Energies.

Energy is the only life, and is from the Body; and Reason is the bound or outward circumference of Energy.

Energy is Eternal Delight.

Such is the form taken towards 1793 by the *Marriage of Heaven and Hell*, which proposed that instead of turning away from Evil, man should look it boldly in the face. In these conditions there was no possibility of coming to rest. The Eternal Delight is at the same time the Eternal Awakening. It is perhaps the Hell which Heaven could never truly reject.

In Blake's life the joy of the senses was a touchstone. Sensuality set him against the primacy of reason. He condemned the moral law in the name of sensuality. 'As the caterpillar chooses the fairest leaves to lay her eggs on,' he wrote, 'so the priest lays his curse on the fairest joys.' He resolutely called for sensual happiness, for the exuberance of the body. 'The lust of the goat is the bounty of God,' he said, and 'The nakedness of woman is the work of God.'[12] And yet William Blake's sensuality was very different from that subterfuge which denies true sensuality by seeing it solely as health. Blake's sensuality was on the side of Energy, which is Evil, which restores it to its deepest significance. If nakedness is the work of God – if the lust of the goat is His bounty – it is the wisdom of Hell that heralds this truth. He wrote:

> In a wife I would desire
> What in whores is always found –
> The lineaments of Gratified desire.[13]

Elsewhere he expressed that burst of energy, the violence, which he believed Evil to be. The following poem is like the account of a dream:

> I saw a chapel all of gold
> That none did dare to enter in,
> And many weeping stood without,
> Weeping, mourning, worshipping.
>
> I saw a serpent rise between
> The white pillars of the door,
> And he forc'd & forc'd & forc'd,
> Down the golden hinges tore.
>
> And along the pavement sweet,
> Set with pearls & rubies bright,
> All his slimy length he drew,
> Till upon the altar white
>
> Vomiting his poison out
> On the bread & on the wine.
> So I turn'd into a sty
> And laid me down among the swine.[14]

Blake was surely aware of the significance of this poem. The golden chapel can doubtless be equated with the 'Garden of love' in *Songs of Experience*, with ' "Thou shalt not" writ over the door.'

Blake's mind was open to the truth of Evil which exists beyond sensuality and the feeling of horror which is connected with it. This appears in *The Tyger*, a poem that has now become a classic. A few words of this poem are the very opposite of a subterfuge. Never have eyes as wide open as these stared at the sun of cruelty.

Tyger! Tyger! burning bright
In the forests of the night,
What immortal hand or eye
Could frame thy fearful symmetry?

What the hammer? what the chain?
In what furnace was thy brain?
What the anvil? what dread grasp
Dare its deadly terrors clasp?

When the stars threw down their spears,
And water'd heaven with their tears,
Did he smile his work to see?
Did he who made the Lamb make thee?[15]

In Blake's stare I sense both resolution and fear. I also feel that it is difficult to penetrate the abyss which man is for himself more deeply than in this representation of Evil:

Cruelty has a Human Heart,
And Jealousy a Human Face;
Terror the Human Form Divine,
And Secrecy the Human Dress.

The Human Dress is forged Iron,
The Human Form a fiery Forge,
The Human Face a Furnace seal'd,
The Human Heart its hungry Gorge.[16]

BLAKE AND THE FRENCH REVOLUTION

This form of excess does not reveal the mystery connected with it. No-one can elucidate it. The feelings behind it elude us. We are left with an insoluble contradiction. By affirming Evil Blake was affirming liberty, but the liberty of Evil is also the negation of liberty. We cannot begin to solve this contradiction, so how could Blake? He rebelliously called the Revolution the power of the people, yet he exalted the blind release of brute force, thinking that the blindness of it corresponded to a divine form of excess. In the *Proverbs of Hell* we read that 'the wrath of the lion is the wisdom of God', and 'the roaring of lions, the howling of wolves, the raging of the stormy sea, and the destructive sword, are portions of eternity too great for the eye of man.'

'The roaring of lions' awakens us to the feeling of the impossible: nothing can give it a sense acceptable to the human mind. All we can do is to wake up without ever hoping to sleep again. Not only will the confusion of the epics no longer matter, but, as we try to escape from it, we pass from waking and awareness of the confusion, to the sleep of logical explanation. What mattered for Blake was that which excluded reduction to the dimensions of the *possible*; what mattered for him was that which was 'too great for the eye of man' . What meaning had God for him if not an awakening to the feeling of the *impossible*?

It may seem meaningless to talk of the lion, the wolf or the tiger, but these wild beasts, in which Blake saw 'portions of eternity', announce that which awakens us, that which the sleepy movement of language conceals, for language substitutes the appearance of a solution for the insoluble, and a screen for violent truth. In short, any commentary which does not simply say that commentaries are useless and impossible moves us away from the truth at the very moment when it might come close to it in itself. It interposes a screen which subdues the light – and even what I say is yet another obstacle which we must remove if we want to *see*.[17]

The poems published by Blake in 1794, like *The Tyger*, express his reactions to the Terror. *A Divine Image* was etched as heads were rolling. The following passage from *Europe*, written at the same time, is a more direct evocation of the Terror. The divinity of passion which merges with Luvah under the name of Orc and which incarnates revolutions is evoked in a burst of flames:

... And in the vineyards of red France appear'd the
light of his fury.
The sun glow'd fiery red!
The furious terrors flew around
On Golden chariots raging with red wheels dropping
with blood!
The Lions lash their wrathful tails!
The Tigers couch upon the prey & suck the ruddy
tide.[18]

Nothing can be drawn from these outbursts, this turmoil of death, that a non-poetic language could express. At best discussion is banal. The worst eludes even poetry: nervous depression alone can reach it. Yet poetry – the poetic vision – is not submitted to common reduction. Besides, in Blake the revolutionary idea contrasted love with hatred, Liberty with Right and Duty. He never gave it the features of Urizen, the symbol of Reason and Authority, the expression of the absence of love. This does not lead to any coherent attitude. It leads solely to poetic disorder. If the Revolution acts according to the dictates of Reason it moves away from disorder but it also loses that incongruous, provocative innocence, containing a welter of opposites and heralded by the figure of Blake.

In times of historical transformation such disorders, however infinite their significance, cast no more than a furtive light, which has nothing to do with the true movements of history. Through a succession of ingenuous contradictions, however, this light conciliates, for a brief instant, these movements with the very depths of all time.

If it were not revolutionary and did not have the speed of lightning it would show us nothing outside the opacity of the present, but at the same time it would be unable to adapt itself to the requirements of a revolution which changes the world. Would this necessary reservation cancel that significance I have mentioned? It may be barely perceptible, but if it is the significance of Blake, it is that of a man who rejects the limitations imposed upon him. Has the human being ever, for a single second, been able to discover an expression of liberty which rises above misery? In an eloquent world where logic reduces each thing to a certain order, William Blake spoke, on his own, the language of the Bible or the Vedas. By so doing he managed to restore life to original energy. So the truth of Evil which is essentially a rejection of subservience, is his truth. He is *one of us*, singing in the tavern and laughing with the children. He is never a 'sad sire', moralising and rational, who looks after himself and his money and slowly yields to the sadness of logic, without *energy*.

The moralist condemns the energy which he lacks. There is no doubt that humanity had to go through this phase. How could it survive if it had not denounced an excess of energy, if the very number of those who lacked energy had not brought those who had too much of it to their senses? But the necessity of adapting oneself ultimately demands a return to innocence. The marvellous indifference and childishness of William Blake, his feeling of ease when confronted with the impossible, his anguish which left boldness intact, all his defects and qualities were the expression of a simpler age and marked a return to lost innocence. Even a paradoxical form of Christianity can serve to indicate this; he is the only man to have seized with both hands, from two extremes, the roundabout of all times. Everything within him came to a halt before the necessity which entails laborious activity in a factory. He could not reply to the cold face animated by the pleasure of discipline. This sage, whose wisdom was close to folly, who was never disheartened by the work on which his liberty depended, did not have the self-effacement of those who 'understand', who surrender, renouncing victory. His energy rejected concessions to the spirit of work. His writings have a festive turbulence which gives the feelings he expressed a sense of laughter and liberty run loose. He never pursed his lips. The horror of his mythological poems is there to liberate us, not to flatten us: it reveals the great momentum of the universe. It calls for energy, never for depression.

Blake has given a faithful image of this incongruous liberty animated by the energy of all times in an incomparable poem about Klopstock, whom he despised. In it he refers to himself in the third person singular.

> When Klopstock England defied,
> Uprose William Blake in his pride;
> For old Nobodaddy aloft
> Farted & Belch'd & cough'd;
> Then swore a great oath that made heaven quake,
> And call'd aloud to English Blake.
> Blake was giving his body ease
> At Lambeth beneath the poplar trees.
> From his seat then started he,
> And turned him round three times three.
> The Moon at that sight blush'd scarlet red,
> The stars threw down their cups & fled.[19]

NOTES

1. In France, William Blake, the visionary painter and poet, has only recently been appreciated by a very few people. There is no doubt that the religious element in his life and work has counted against him, and the French reading public has proved incapable of grasping the significance of this element. I am amazed that so little store should have been set by Blake's relationship with surrealism. That curious piece, *An Island in the Moon*, is hardly known.

2. His visions, which he spoke of familiarly, his linguistic excesses, the delirious atmosphere of his pictures and poems, all contributed to the image of Blake as a lunatic. But this was a superficial impression. We have the evidence of people who met him and at first took him for a lunatic, but soon readily acknowledged that he was no such thing. Nevertheless, even while these people were alive, the legend that the visionary had spent thirty years in a lunatic asylum grew. This legend was based on an article which appeared in the *Revue Britannique* in Paris in 1833 (3e série, t.iv, p. 183-186).

> The two most celebrated inmates of the asylum of Bedlam [writes the anonymous author] are the incendiary Martin... and Blake, nicknamed the *Seer*. When I had examined this entire populace of criminals and lunatics, I asked to visit Blake's cell. He was a tall, pale man of great eloquence; in all the annals of demonology nothing is more extraordinary than Blake's visions. He was not the victim of a mere hallucination; he believed deeply in the truth of his visions, he conversed with Michelangelo and dined with Semiramis... This man was believed to be the painter of Ghosts... When I entered his cell, he was drawing a flea whose ghost, so he maintained, had just appeared to him.

Blake did indeed draw the ghost of the flea in question. The drawing, entitled *The Ghost of a Flea*, hangs in the Tate Gallery. Had we not a detailed knowledge and a day to day account of Blake's life which would seem to exclude a sojourn, however brief, in Bedlam, we might have taken the account in the *Revue Britannique* seriously. But Mona Wilson has traced its source. The writer in the *Revue Britannique* plagiarised an article published in March 1833 by the *Monthly Magazine*. Like the *Revue Britannique*, the *Monthly Magazine* mentions Blake the visionary and Martin the incendiary, but only that part of the account referring to Martin is set in Bedlam. The author of the *Revue Britannique* has simply placed both the individuals mentioned in the article he plagiarised in Bedlam. In Mona Wilson's *The Life of William Blake*, [London, Rupert Hart-Davis] we have the English and the French version of the two articles. The time has come to explode this myth. Yet, in 1875, an article in the *Cornhill Magazine* still referred to the thirty years Blake had spent in a lunatic asylum.

3. W. P. Witcutt, *Blake, A psychological study*, London, Hollis & Carter, 1946.
4. William Blake, *Poetry and Prose*, edited by Geoffrey Keynes, London, Nonesuch Press, 1927.
5. Quoted in W. P. Witcutt, op. cit.
6. William Blake, op. cit.
7. *All religions are one*, etched about 1788, in William Blake, op. cit. Compare 'All [men] are alike in the Poetic Genius' with Lautréamont's 'Poetry must be made by all, not by one.'
8. Submitted to material ends, which are frequently those of selfish individuals.
9. William Blake, *Poèmes choisis*, traduits par M.-L. Cazamian, Aubier, 1944, Introduction.
10. William Blake, *Poetry and Prose*.
11. Ibid.
12. Ibid.
13. Ibid.
14. Ibid. It would be hard to give a better description of the

sexual act in as far as it is the sacrilegious transgression of a taboo. The poem which follows in the collection shows us the exact meaning of the quotation:

> I asked a thief to steal me a peach:
> He turned up his eyes.
> I asked a lithe lady to lie her down:
> Holy & meek she cries.
> As soon as I went an angel came:
> He wink'd at the thief
> And smil'd at the dame,
> And without one word spoke
> Had a peach from the tree,
> And 'twixt earnest & joke
> Enjoy'd the Lady.

15. Ibid.

16. Ibid. The title of the two verses is *A Divine Image*. The first was based on another with a very different meaning (by a process which reminds us of Lautréamont, though Lautréamont always based himself on the words of other writers, while Blake based himself on his own:

> For Mercy has a human heart,
> Pity a human face,
> And Love, the human form divine,
> And Peace, the human dress.

These lines are from the poem entitled *The Divine Image*, in *Songs of Innocence*, earlier, therefore, than *Songs of Experience*, which were written in 1794. For Blake the reunion of these two poems in 1794 indicated the two contrary states of the human soul).

17. Jean Wahl has written about *The Tyger* in his *Notes sur William Blake* (in *Poésie, Pensée, Perception, Calmann-Lévy, 1948.*

> The Tiger is the divine spark, fierce individuality surrounded by the forest where good and evil are intermixed. But should the consciousness which we have of this terrible beauty make us accept evil

without transforming it? And if there is a possible transformation where should we look for it and how should we effect it? The last lines are an answer to this problem. The spark itself is a shaft of the great light which unifies and cures, a burst of divine humanity. There is not only beauty but good in terrible things.

This outburst is, as Wahl said, subdued. The last lines are: 'Tyger! Tyger! burning bright / In the forests of the night, / What immortal hand or eye, / Dare frame thy fearful symmetry?' But further on, p. 19-23, Jean Wahl himself leads us to understand that he considers the importance of commentaries extremely doubtful: he talks of the 'non-Blakian art, that art which Blake almost cursed, of intellectual analysis.' He concludes one article (*William Blake païen, chrétien et mystique* dans *William Blake, 1757-1827*. Catalogue de l'Exposition Blake à la Galerie Drouin, 1947) with the words: 'The emanations put out every light and clasp each other without asking their name.' Blake himself had said: 'The tygers of wrath are wiser than the horses of instruction'.

18. William Blake, *Poetry and Prose*.
19. Ibid.

SADE

In the midst of this rowdy imperial epic we see a blasted head flashing, a massive chest crossed by lightning, the phallus-man, an august and cynical profile grimacing like a ghastly and sublime Titan; we feel a thrill of the infinite in the accursed pages, the breath of a tempestuous ideal vibrating on these burnt lips. Come nearer and you will hear the arteries of the universal soul, veins swollen with divine blood palpitating in this muddy and bleeding carcass. This cloaca is impregnated with azure, there is a God-like element in these latrines. Close your ear to the rattle of bayonets and the bark of cannon; turn your eye from this moving tide of war, of victories or defeats; then you will see a huge ghost bursting out against the shadows; you will see the vast and sinister figure of the Marquis de Sade appear above a whole epoch sewn with stars.

Swinburne

Why should a period of revolution lend a lustre to the arts and the world of letters? Armed violence is ill matched with the enrichment of a domain which can only be enjoyed in peacetime. The newspapers show man's destiny in all its horror. It is the town itself, not the heroes of tragedies and novels, which gives the mind the thrill that imaginary figures usually provide for us. Any immediate vision of life is poor compared to the one elaborated by the reflection and the art of the historian. But if the same applies to love, whose intelligible truth lies in memory (so much so that the loves of mythical heroes usually seem more true to us than our own) is it true to say that the moment of conflagration, even when it is imperfectly revealed by our purblind consciousness, absorbs us entirely? A time of rebellion is basically unfavourable to the development of the arts. At first sight the Revolution is a sterile period in French literature. One important exception can be advanced, but it concerns an unrecognised man – who, when alive, had a reputation, but a bad one: Sade's case, because it is so exceptional, would seem to confirm such sterility rather than to contradict it.

To begin with it must be said that the recognition of Sade's genius and of the beauty and significance of his work is recent. The writings of Jean Paulhan, Pierre Klossowski and Maurice Blanchot have confirmed it. Never before have such splendid homages contributed to the slow but sure establishment of Sade's reputation.[1]

SADE AND THE STORMING OF THE BASTILLE

Sade's life and work are indeed connected with historical events, but in the strangest possible way. The sense of the revolution is not 'given' in his ideas: if there is any connection it is more like that between the uneven components of some unfinished figure – between a ruin and some rock, or between the night and silence. Though the features of this figure remain confused, the time has come to distinguish them.

Few events have a greater symbolic value than the

storming of the Bastille. During the feast which com-
memorates it, many Frenchmen feel something which
unites them to the sovereignty of their country as they
watch a torchlight tattoo advance through the dark. This
popular sovereignty, which is both turbulent and rebellious, is as irresistible as a cry. There is no better symbol of
festivity than the insurrectional destruction of a prison.
Festivity, which is sovereign by definition, is the very
essence of release, from which inflexible sovereignty stems.
But were it to lack an element of chance, were it to lack
caprice, the event would not have the same importance: it
is because of this that it is symbolic, because of this that it
differs from abstract formulae.

It has been said that the storming of the Bastille did not
really have the importance which has been attributed to it.
This is possible. On 14 July, 1789, there were no prisoners
of any note. The event may have been based on a
misunderstanding, a misunderstanding which, according
to Sade, he himself had created. But we could say that this
equivocal element gives the whole episode that blind,
almost unknown quality, without which it would have
been no more than a response to the dictates of necessity, as
in a factory. Caprice, or chance, not only partially deny the
interest aroused by 14 July: they also give it an adventitious
interest.

At the time when the people decided on an event that
was to shake, if not to deliver, the world, one of the
unfortunate prisoners in the Bastille was the author of
Justine, a book in the introduction of which[2] Jean Paulhan
assures us that it *presented such a serious problem that it took over
a century to reply to it*. Sade had then been in prison for ten
years and in the Bastille since 1784. He was one of the most
rebellious and furious men ever to have talked of rebellion
and fury; he was, in a word, a monster, obsessed by the idea
of an *impossible* liberty. The manuscript of *Justine* was still

in the Bastille on 14 July, but, like the manuscript of *Les Cent Vingt Journées de Sodome*, it had been abandoned in an empty cell.

We know that Sade harangued the crowd the day before the insurrection. He appears to have employed the pipe used for emptying his dirty water as a loud speaker and one of his many provocative actions was to yell out that the prisoners were being slaughtered.[3] This is in keeping with the provocative nature of his entire life and work. But the man who had been in chains for ten years for having been fury incarnate and who had been awaiting his release for as long a time was not released by the 'fury' of the mob. It often happens that a dream allows us an anguished glimpse of a perfect possibility which it reveals at the last moment, as if a confused reply were the only one *capricious* enough to satisfy an exasperated desire. The prisoner's exasperation retarded his release for nine months. The governor requested that Sade, who was so clearly in agreement with the insurgents, be transferred.[4] When the lock gave way and the mob filled the corridors, his cell was empty. The turmoil resulted in the loss of the Marquis' scattered manuscripts. *Les Cent Vingt Journées de Sodome*, the first book to express the true fury which man holds within him and which he has to control and conceal, the book that can be said to dominate all books, disappeared. Instead of liberating its author, the mob at the Bastille lost the manuscript which was the first expression of the full horror of liberty.

14 July was truly a liberation, but in the cryptic sense of a dream. The manuscript was found much later, and was published in our own time, but the Marquis himself was dispossessed of it. He believed it was lost for ever, and this filled him with despair. It was, he wrote, 'the greatest misfortune that heaven had prepared for him.'[5] He died unaware that what he thought was irremediably lost

would find its place, a little later, among the 'imperishable monuments of the past.'

THE WILL OF SELF-DESTRUCTION

We see that an author and a book are not always the products of a period of tranquillity. In this case everything is connected with the violence of a revolution, and the figure of the Marquis de Sade only belongs in a very distant way to the history of literature. He admittedly wanted to enter it like anyone else and despaired at the loss of his manuscripts. But nobody is entitled to desire and to hope lucidly for what Sade desired obscurely and obtained: the staging of not only the objects and the victims (who are merely there in order to satisfy the mania for denial), but of the author and the work itself. It is possible that the fate which willed Sade to write, and to be dispossessed of his work, has an element of truth similar to that in his work – it contains the bad news of a conciliation between the living and that which kills them, between Good and Evil, and, we might almost say, between the loudest cry and silence. We cannot know what impulse a man as fickle as he obeyed when he inserted the instructions concerning his tomb in his will. He wanted it to be in the corner of his land – but these relentless words, whatever the reason he wrote them, dominate and terminate his life:

> Once the grave has been filled in, it must be sown with acorns so that, in the future, the ground will again be covered with vegetation, the copse will be as thick as it was before, and the traces of my tomb will disappear from the surface of the earth as I hope my memory will vanish from the memory of men.[6]

Indeed, the distance between the 'tears of blood' wept for *Les Cent Vingt Journées de Sodome* and this demand for nothingness is no greater than that between the arrow and the target. I shall later show that the true sense of an infinitely profound work is to be found in the author's desire to disappear, to vanish without leaving a human trace, because nothing else is worthy of him.

SADE'S THOUGHT

Let this be clear: nothing would be more fruitless than to take Sade literally, seriously. From whichever angle we approach him, he eludes us. Of the various philosophies he attributes to his characters we cannot retain a single one. Klossowski's study has proved it. Through the creatures of the novel, he at times elaborates a theology of the *supremely wicked Being*. At other times he is an atheist, but not a cold-blooded one: his atheism defies God and battens on sacrilege; it usually substitutes *Nature in a state of perpetual motion* for God. On still other occasions he is devout, on others a blasphemer. 'Her barbarous hand,' says the chemist Almani, 'can only create evil: so evil amuses her: and I am expected to love such a mother! No! I shall imitate her, but I shall hate her. I shall copy her: it is she who wills it, but I shall detest her at the same time.'[7]

   The key to these contradictions is to be found in a passage which contains the essence of Sade's thought, taken from a letter of 26 January, 1782, written 'from the *poulailler* (the dungeon) of Vincennes' and signed 'Des Aulnets' – as if Sade's true name were incompatible with a moral assertion: 'O man!' he exclaimed, 'Is it for you to say what is good or what is evil?... You want to analyse the laws of nature and your heart... your heart whereon they are engraved, is itself an enigma which you cannot solve...'[8] He could never actually come to rest and there were few principles which he firmly maintained. Though he was certainly a materialist, this did not solve his problem: that of the Evil which he loved, and of the Good which condemned it. Indeed, Sade, who loved Evil, whose entire work was intended to make Evil desirable, was unable either to condemn or to justify it. In his own way each of the debauched philosophers he portrayed, tempted him, but they did not, and could not, find a principle which elicits the accursed quality from those actions whose benefits they praised. It is this same accursed quality which they sought in these actions. And Almani's bitter exclamation proves that he could only give his thoughts an uncertain and troubled course. The only point about which Sade was sure was that nothing deserved punishment – or at least human punishment. 'The law,' he said[9] 'cold in itself, can never be accessible to those passions which can justify the cruel act of murder.'

Sade never swerved in his belief in this profoundly significant creed. 'You want,' he wrote in a letter of 29 January, 1782, 'the whole universe to be virtuous and you do not feel that everything would perish in an instant if there were nothing but virtues on earth... You do not want to understand that, since vice must exist, it is as unjust of you to punish it as it would be to poke fun at a blind man...' And further on: 'Enjoy yourself, my friend, enjoy yourself and do not pass judgement... enjoy yourself, I say, leave to nature the care of moving you as she pleases and to eternity that of punishing you.'[10] If the 'release' of the passions is accursed, punishment, which wants to obviate them, has an element which crime lacks. (The moderns say, with greater precision, that the crime ordained by passion may be dangerous but is no less authentic. This does not apply to repression, which is subordinate to the condition of seeking what is useful, rather than what is authentic.)

Many people will agree that the act of the judge has an

icy quality which, with its lack of passion or of any element of risk, closes the heart. But once we have acknowledged this and placed Sade resolutely before the judge, we must admit that he had neither the consistency nor the rigour which allows us to reduce his life to any one principle. He was boundlessly generous: we know that he saved the Montreuils from the scaffold and that Madame de Montreuil, his mother-in-law, had had a *lettre de cachet* issued against him. But he had agreed to this, and had almost begged her to eliminate by the same means Nanon Sablonnière, his servant who had seen too much.[11] Between 1792 and 1793 he had proved himself to be a fervent republican at the Section des Piques, of which he was secretary and president. Nevertheless we should recall a letter of 1791 in which he wrote:

You ask me what my real feelings are so that you can follow them. Nothing was as tactful as that part of your letter, but it will be with the greatest difficulty that I shall reply to your question. First, as a man of letters, the obligation I am under to work each day, either for one party or for the other, establishes a mobility in my opinions which is reflected in my innermost thoughts. Do I really want to fathom them? They favour no party and are a mixture of them all. I am anti-Jacobin, I hate them heartily, I adore the king but abhor the old abuses; I love a mass of articles in the constitution, but others repel me. I want their lustre to be returned to the nobility because I can see no point in taking it away. I want the king to be head of the state: I do not want a national assembly but two chambers, as in England, which gives the king a mitigated authority, balanced by half of the nation, necessarily divided into two orders: the third is useless, I shall have none of it. That is what I think.

What am I? An aristocrat or a democrat? You tell me,
if you please... for I am unable to judge.[12]

We obviously cannot deduce anything from this letter,
written to a bourgeois who was of assistance to him in
collecting his rents, except for a 'mobility in my opinions'
and the 'What am I?' which the *divin marquis* might well
have taken as his motto.[13]

It seems to me that in his studies, *Sade et la Révolution* or
Esquisse du système de Sade, Pierre Klossowski has painted a
somewhat contrived portrait of the author of *Justine*; it is
nothing but an elaborate system in which, by a clever use of
dialectics, he has endeavoured to implicate God, theo-
cratic society and the revolt of a *grand seigneur* who wants to
retain his privileges and deny his obligations. In one sense
Klossowski's studies are very Hegelian, but they lack
Hegel's rigour. *The Phenomenology of Mind*, to which such
dialectics bear a resemblance, constitutes a circular whole
embracing the entire development of the mind in history.
But Klossowski draws too hasty a conclusion from a
brilliant passage in *La Philosophie dans le Boudoir*, where
Sade claimed to base the republican state on crime. To
proceed to substitute the king's execution for the execution
of God is indeed tempting – a sociological concept based on
theology, guided by psychoanalysis, and clinging to the
ideas of Joseph de Maistre. Yet all this is a little fragile. The
words attributed by Sade to Dolmancé are no more than a
logical indication, one of a thousand proofs given of the
errors of a humanity which has not committed itself to
destruction and Evil. In the end Klossowski goes as far as to
say that Dolmancé's reasoning might only be there in order
to prove the falsity of the republican principle. Yet the
marquis turned his back on so many worthy guesses: the
true problem is very different.

'When I look about me and see so many writers,' wrote

Jean Paulhan,[14] 'so devoted to the rejection of literary artifice in favour of an event which can hardly be recounted, which, we are reminded, is both erotic and terrifying – writers constantly eager to take the opposite course to that of Creativity and determined to find the sublime in the infamous, greatness in subversion, who demand that every work should commit and compromise its author for ever . . . I wonder whether we should not see, in so extensive a terror, a memory, rather than an invention or an ideal. I wonder whether modern literature, in what seems to me its most living form, or at all events its most aggressive form, is not entirely orientated towards the past and determined by Sade . . . ' Paulhan may be wrong in attributing imitators to Sade – we talk about him, admire him, but nobody feels that he should be like him: we dream of other 'terrors'. Yet Paulhan has defined Sade's position admirably. He was not concerned with the possibilities or the dangers of language. He could not imagine his work independently of the object he depicted, because his object possessed him – in the devil's sense of the word. He wrote lost in the desire for the object and applied himself like a monk. Klossowski rightly says:[15]

> Sade not only dreamed. He guided the dream back to the object which started him dreaming with the accomplished method of a contemplative monk who sets his soul in prayer before the divine mystery. The Christian soul grows conscious of itself before God. But if the romantic soul, which is no more than a nostalgic state of faith,[16] grows conscious of itself when it presents its passion as an absolute, so that the pathetic state becomes a function of living, Sade's soul only grew conscious of itself through the object which exasperated its virility and which constituted it in a state of exasperated virility that also became a

paradoxical function of living. It only felt itself living in exasperation.

At this point we must add that the object in question, though comparable to God (Klossowski, as a Christian, is the first to draw the comparison), is not given as God is for the man who prays. The object as such (a human being) would still be indifferent – it must be modified so that the necessary suffering should be obtained from it. To modify it means to destroy it.

I shall later demonstrate that Sade (and in this he differs from the normal sadist, who is instinctive) had as his goal the clear consciousness of what can only be attained by 'release' – though release leads to the loss of consciousness. That is to say that he had as his goal the clear consciousness of suppression – of the difference between subject and object. Thus his goal only differed from that of philosophy by the path he chose in order to attain it: Sade started with an examination of violent 'releases' in practice which he wanted to make intelligible, while philosophy starts from a calm consciousness – from distinct intelligibility – in order to bring it to a point of fusion.

To begin with I shall discuss the evident monotony of Sade's books which is due to the decision to subordinate literature to the expression of an inexpressible event. These books, it is true, differ no less from what is usually considered to be literature than a stretch of colourless desert rocks differs from the varied landscape full of brooks and lakes and fields which we love. But how long will it take us to measure the size or to assess the greatness of that stretch of rocks?

SADE'S FRENZY

Sade, who cut himself off from humanity, only had one occupation in his long life which really absorbed him – that of enumerating to the point of exhaustion the possibilities of destroying human beings, of destroying them and of enjoying the thought of their death and suffering. Even the most beautiful description would have had little meaning for him. Interminable and monotonous enumeration alone managed to present him with the void, the desert, for which he yearned, and which his books still present to the reader.

Boredom seeps from the monstrosity of Sade's work, but it is this very boredom which constitutes its significance. As the Christian Klossowski says, his endless novels are more like prayer books than books of entertainment. The accomplished technique behind them is that of the 'monk... who sets his soul in prayer before the divine mystery'. One must read them as they were written, with the intention of fathoming a mystery which is no less profound, nor perhaps less 'divine', than that of theology. This man, who appears in his letters as unstable, facetious, beguiling, fanatical, enamoured or amused, capable of tenderness and even of remorse, contented himself, in his books, with an invariable exercise in which an acute but permanent tension, infinitely sustained, springs from the cares that limit us. From the outset we are lost on inaccessible heights. Nothing remains that is hesitant or moderative. In an endless and relentless tornado, the objects of desire are invariably propelled towards torture and death. The only conceivable end is possible desire of the executioner to be the victim of torture himself. In Sade's will, to which we have already referred, this instinct reached its climax by demanding that not even his tomb should survive: it led to the wish that his very name should 'vanish from the memory of men.'

If we see such violence as the symbol of a difficult truth which obsessed him who followed it to such a degree that he came to regard it as a mystery, we must connect it with the image Sade himself gave of it.

He wrote at the beginning of *Les Cent Vingt Journées de Sodome*:[17]

> It is now, friendly reader, that you must prepare your heart and mind for the most impure story that has ever been told since the world began, a similar book not existing either amongst the ancients or the moderns. Imagine that every honest pleasure – or any pleasure permitted by that beast which you always talk of, though you are not acquainted with it, and which you call nature – imagine, I say, that these pleasures will be deliberately excluded from this collection and that if you find them by any chance it will only be because they are accompanied by some crime or coloured by some infamy.

Sade's aberration went as far as to turn his heroes into cowards rather than villains. Here is the description of one of them:

'False, hard, imperious, barbarous, selfish, prodigal in his own pleasures and avaricious whenever he might make himself useful, lying, greedy, drunken, cowardly, incestuous, a sodomite, a murderer, an incendiary, a thief...'
This is the Duc de Blangis, one of the four executioners of *Les Cent Vingt Journées de Sodome*. 'A determined child would have terrified this colossus and once he could no longer use cunning or treachery to get rid of his enemy, he became timid and cowardly.'

Of the four villains Blangis is by no means the worst.

> Président de Curval was the dean of the society. Almost sixty years of age and singularly ravaged by debauch, he was little more than a skeleton. He was tall, thin, with hollow, faded eyes, a pale, unhealthy

mouth, raised chin and long nose. As hairy as a satyr, with a flat back and soft buttocks which looked more like dirty rags falling from the top of his thighs... Curval was so deep in the mire of vice and dissipation that it had become impossible for him to talk about anything else. He always had the filthiest expressions on his lips as in his heart, and he interspersed them with blasphemies caused by the true horror which he and his colleagues felt for anything to do with religion. The derangement of his mind, further increased by continual drunkenness, had given him for some years an air of imbecility and debasement which was, he claimed, one of his greatest joys.

'Foul from head to foot', even 'evil-smelling', Président de Curval was 'completely debased', while the Duc de Blangis incarnated splendour and violence.

If he was violent in his desires, what did he become, Great God!, when intoxicated by lust? He was no longer a man, he was an enraged tiger. Unfortunate whoever served his passions! Appalling cries, atrocious blasphemies burst forth from his swollen heart, flames seemed to spring from his eyes, he foamed and neighed and behaved like a veritable God of lewdness.

Sade did not possess this unlimited cruelty. He frequently had trouble with the police, who viewed him with suspicion but could not charge him with any real crime. We know that he slashed a young beggar, Rose Keller, with a penknife and poured hot wax into her wounds. The castle of Lacoste in Provence appears to have been the scene of organised orgies, but without those excesses which Sade had devised for the castle of Silling, isolated, as he liked to represent it, in a rocky wilderness. A passion which he may sometimes have cursed meant that the sight of other people suffering excited him to the point of insanity. In an official statement Rose Keller spoke of the appalling cries which accompanied his orgasm. This characteristic, at least, he shared with Blangis. I do not know if we are justified in associating these outbursts with mere pleasure. After a certain point, excess can no longer be gauged. Does one talk of pleasure when a savage hangs himself to a rope by a hook dug into his chest and flies around a stake? From the evidence in Marseilles we see that the Marquis tore his flesh with whips whose thongs were edged with pins. Indeed, we must go still further. Sade's fantasies were such that some of them would disgust the most hardened fakir. If anyone pretended to admire the life led by the villains of Silling, he would be boasting. Next to them Benoist Labre[18] appears fastidious. There is no ascetic who has surpassed the limits of disgust to such an extent.

FROM RELEASE TO A CLEAR CONSCIOUSNESS

But such was Sade's moral position. He was very different from his heroes in that he frequently displayed human feelings, and he experienced states of release and ecstasy which seemed to him of great significance with regard to common possibilities. He did not think that he could, or should, cut out of his life these dangerous states to which his insurmountable desires led him. Instead of forgetting about them, as one usually does, he dared to look them in the face in his moments of normality, and to ask himself that unfathomable question which they raise for all men. Others before him had had the same lapses, but there was a fundamental distinction between the release of passion and clear consciousness.

Never had the human mind ceased to correspond, on

occasion, to the requisites that lead to sadism. But this happened furtively, in the darkness which springs from the incompatibility between violence, which is blind, and the lucidity of consciousness. Frenzy banished consciousness. Consciousness, on the other hand, in its agonised condemnation, denied and ignored the significance of frenzy. In the solitude of his prison Sade was the first man to give a rational expression to those uncontrollable desires, on the negation of which consciousness has based the social structure and the very image of man. It was in order to do this that he had to question every value which had hitherto been considered absolute. His books give us the feeling that, by an exasperated inversion, he wanted the impossible and the *reverse* of life. He was as decisive as a housewife who skins a rabbit hurriedly and deftly (the housewife also reveals the reverse of the truth, and in this case, the reverse is also the heart of the truth).

Sade based himself on a common experience. Sensuality, which liberated from ordinary constraints, is aroused not only by the presence, but by a modification of the possible object. In other words an erotic impulse, which is a release (as far as the performance of work and propriety in general are concerned), is sparked off by the concordant release of its object. 'The secret is unfortunately only too sure,' observed Sade, 'and there is not a libertine anchored in vice who is not acquainted with the power effect murder has on the senses... ' 'So it is true,' exclaims Blangis, 'that crime in itself has such an attraction that, independently of lust, it alone can inflame the passions.'

An object of passion cannot always be actively released. That which destroys a being, also releases him: besides, release is always the ruin of a being who has set limitations on his propriety. Revelation itself breaks these limitations (it is the sign of the disorder produced by the object which yields to it). Sexual disorder discomposes the coherent forms which establish us, for ourselves and for others, as defined beings - it moves them into an infinity which is death. There is a turmoil, a sense of drowning, in sensuality which is similar to the stench of corpses. On the other hand, in the anguish of death, something is lost and eludes us, a disorder begins within us, an impression of emptiness, and the state which we enter is similar to that which precedes a sensual desire. There was once a young man who could not attend a burial without experiencing a physical thrill, and he therefore had to leave his father's funeral procession. His conduct differed from ordinary behaviour. But we cannot reduce sexual desire to that which is agreeable and beneficent. There is in it an element of disorder and excess which goes as far as to endanger the life of whoever indulges in it.

In Sade's imagination this disorder and this excess were carried to extremes. Nobody, unless he is totally deaf to it, can finish *Les Cent Vingt Journées de Sodome* without feeling sick: the sickest is he who is sexually excited by the book. The amputated fingers, the eyes, the torn finger nails, the tortures of which moral horror intensifies the pain, the mother induced, by cunning and terror, to murder her son, the cries, the blood and the stench, everything contributes to our nausea. It stifles us and, instead of creating in us a feeling of acute pain, it creates an emotion which discomposes - and kills. How did he dare? How could he? The man who wrote these perverted pages knew, he went as far as the imagination allows: there was nothing respectable which he did not mock, nothing pure which he did not soil, nothing joyful which he did not frighten. Each one of us is personally implicated: however slender the human element in this book, it strikes us as a blasphemy; whatever there is that is precious and holy, it appears to us like a skin disease. But what if he were to go further? Indeed, this book is the only one in which the mind of man is shown *as it really is*. The language of *Les Cent Vingt Journées de Sodome* is that of a universe which degrades gradually and systematically, which tortures and destroys the totality of the beings which it presents.

In the bewilderment of sensuality man performs a mental process by which he is equal to what he is. The course of human life inclines us to facile opinions: we represent ourselves as well-defined entities. Nothing seems more secure than the ego which is at the basis of thought. And when it strikes an object it modifies it for its own use: it is never the equal of what is not itself. What is outside our finite beings sometimes subordinates us and becomes an impenetrable infinity. At other times it becomes the object which we handle, which is subordinated to us. Let us add that the individual, by assimilating the things he handles, can still subordinate himself to a finite order which *rivets* him within an immensity. If he then tries to reduce this immensity to scientific laws (which place an equals sign between the world and finite things), he is only equal to his object if he *rivets* himself to an order which crushes him (which denies him – which denies that which differs in him from the finite and subordinate thing). There is only one means in his power to escape from these various limitations – the destruction of a being similar to ourselves. In this destruction the limitations of our fellow human beings are denied; we cannot destroy an inert object: it changes but does not disappear: only a being similar to ourselves disappears, in death. The violence experienced by our fellow human beings is concealed from the order of finite, ultimately useless things. It returns them to immensity.

This was already true in sacrifice. In the horror-ridden apprehension of the sacred, the mind had already sketched the motion by which it becomes equal to *what it is* (to the undefined totality which we cannot know). But sacrifice is nevertheless a fear of release expressed through release. It is the process by which the world of lucid activity (the profane world) liberates itself from a violence which might destroy it. And if it is true that in sacrifice attention is concentrated on a progressive passage of the isolated individual towards the unlimited, it is nevertheless sidetracked towards chance interpretations fully opposed to clear consciousness. Sacrifice is passive, it is based on an elementary fear. Desire alone is active, and desire alone makes us live in the present.

It is only if the mind, confronted by some obstacle, brings its decelerated attention to bear on the object of its desire that lucid consciousness has the opportunity to function. This assumes exasperation and satiety, the recourse to ever more distant possibilities. Finally this presupposes reflection connected with the momentary impossibility of satisfying the desire, and then the taste of satisfying it more consciously.

'True libertines' observed Sade, 'believe that sensations communicated through the auricular organs are the most acute. Consequently our four villains, who wanted their hearts to be as impregnated with lust as they could be, had devised a singular idea for this purpose.' These were the 'story-tellers' who, between the orgies of Silling, had to stimulate the mind by giving accounts of all the vices they had known. They were old prostitutes whose long and sordid experience was the beginning of a perfect image which preceded, and was to be confirmed by, clinical observation. But as far as consciousness is concerned the 'story-tellers' only have one meaning. They give the form of a detailed exposition from a pulpit, objectivised by another voice, to the labyrinth which Sade wished to illuminate until the end. More important still: this singular invention was conceived in the solitude of a cell. The clear and distinct consciousness, for ever renewed and reexamined, of what is at the basis of the erotic instinct, could only form itself in the inhuman conditions of a prison. Had he been free Sade could have satisfied his passion, but prison prevented him. If alleged passion does not torment whoever alleges it, objective, exterior knowledge is possible; but full consciousness is never reached, for full consciousness requires the experience of desire.

Krafft-Ebing's celebrated *Pathologia sexualis*, or other works of the same order, have a significance on the level of an objective awareness of forms of human behaviour, but they remain outside the experience of a profound truth revealed by this behaviour. Such a truth is that of the desire underlying these forms of behaviour, and Krafft-Ebing's rational enumeration does not take it into account. We see that the consciousness of desire is hardly accessible: desire alone alters the clarity of consciousness, but it is above all the possibility of satisfaction which suppresses it. It appears that, for the entire animal kingdom, sexual satisfaction takes place in a 'turmoil of the senses'. The fact that men should have such inhibitions about it, is due to that element which, though not entirely unconscious, is removed from clear consciousness. It was Sade who prepared the way to this consciousness. He never ceased following a line of thought associated with his efforts to assimilate most of the knowledge of his time. But had he not been imprisoned, the disorderly life he led would never have given him the possibility of nurturing an interminable desire which he was unable to satisfy.

The better to emphasise this difficulty I shall add that Sade only announced the fulfilment of consciousness; he could not reach complete clarity. The mind still has to reach, if not the absence of desire, at least that despair left in the reader by the feeling of an ultimate affinity between the desires felt by Sade and his own desires, which are less intense and which are normal.

THE POETRY OF SADE'S DESTINY

We can hardly be surprised that such a strange and difficult truth was first revealed in a splendid and astonishing manner. The possibility of consciousness is its fundamental value, but it could never stop referring to the background which it symbolised. How could this nascent truth have lacked poetic splendour? Without poetic splendour it would never have had its human scope. It is moving to establish that a mythical plot should be connected with that which finally reveals the depths of myths. It took a revolution – the crash of the gates of the Bastille – to deliver Sade's secret to us. He had the misfortune to live this dream, whose obsession is the soul of philosophy, the unity of subject and object. The identity is in the transcendence of the limitations of beings, of the object of desire and the subject which desires. Maurice Blanchot rightly said that Sade 'had managed to make his prison the image of the solitude of the universe', but that this prison, this world, no longer bothered him since he had 'banished all other creatures from it'. Thus the Bastille, where Sade did his writing, was the crucible in which the conscious limitations of being were slowly destroyed by the fire of a passion prolonged by powerlessness.

NOTES

1. We should also mention Swinburne, Baudelaire, Apollinaire, Breton and Eluard, but the patient and tenacious research of Maurice Heine (who died in May 1940) deserves special attention. This beguiling, strange and brilliant individual devoted his life to Sade's memory. This is why we should here recall certain aspects of his personality. When Heine, a bibliophile and a scrupulous scholar (so scrupulous that he hardly published anything) rose to speak at the Congress of Tours (where the Communists split off from the French Socialist Party after the First World War) he fired off his revolver and wounded his wife on the arm. Yet Heine was one of the gentlest, most courteous men I have ever met. This indefatigable defender of Sade was as intractable as his idol and carried his pacifism to its logical conclusions. After taking Lenin's side in 1919 he left the Communist Party in 1921 on account of Trotsky's repression of the anarchist sailors' mutiny in Kronstadt. He squandered his fortune on his research on Sade and died in poverty, eating little in order to feed a vast quantity of cats. He carried his aversion to the death penalty (which he shared with Sade) as far as to condemn bull-fighting. Otherwise he was one of the men who, discreetly but authentically, did the greatest credit to his time. I am proud to have been a friend of his.

2. The first version of the book, written in the Bastille in 1787, was entitled *Les Infortunes de la Vertu*. It is this which has a preface by Jean Paulhan (Sade, *Les Infortunes de la Vertu*, avec une notice de Maurice Heine, une bibliographie de Robert Valençay et une introduction de Jean Paulhan. Ed. de Pont du Jour).

3. *Le Répertoire ou Journalier de la Bastille à commencer le mercredi 15 mai 1782* (published partially by Alfred Bégis, in *La Nouvelle Revue*, November and December 1882) mentions this. Cf. Apollinaire, *L'Oeuvre de Sade*, Paris.

4. This is what, in a letter to the notary Gaufridy, undated but probably written in May 1790, the Marquis de Sade says of himself: 'On 4 July, on account of some little trouble I had caused in the Bastille over some unpleasantness I had been suffering, the governor complained to the minister. I had provoked, they claimed, the people, I had exhorted the mob to overthrow this monument of horror. All this was true.' (*Correspondance inédite du marquis de Sade...* publiée par Paul Bourdin, Paris). And in a letter to the president of the Club de la Constitution de Lacoste, dated 19 April, 1792:

> ask and you will be told whether or not it is universally admitted, whether or not it is actually printed that it was the meetings summoned by me under my windows in the Bastille which caused my sudden removal, like a dangerous individual whose inflammatory proposals were to have this monument of horror overthrown. Obtain the letters from the governor of the Bastille to the minister and when you read the words 'If M. de Sade is not removed from the Bastille this night I will not answer for the king's position' you will see, sir, if I am the man to molest.

(Ibid.) Finally, in the draft of a petition 'to the legislator of the Convention', of 1793:

> I was still in the Bastille on 3 July, 1789. I popularised the garrison; I revealed to the inhabitants of Paris the horrors that were being prepared for them in this castle. Launay thought me dangerous; I am in possession of the letter in which he begs the minister Villedeuil to remove me from a fortress whose treachery I wanted to prevent at all costs.

(Ibid.)
5. Sade said about the matter: 'My manuscripts, for whose loss I weep tears of blood! . . . I will never be able to express my despair at this irreparable loss . . .' (*Correspondance*) And

> manuscripts for which I weep tears of blood each day . . . Forgive me if I do not dwell on this tragedy; it

breaks my heart so cruelly, the best I can do is to try and forget this misfortune and never mention it to anyone. I have found a few things in the areas where the papers of the Bastille were cast, but nothing important... not one single work of consequence... This is the greatest misfortune that heaven has reserved for me...

(Ibid.) Sade did indeed find the second, relatively decent version of *Justine* which he published in 1791. The first, more cryptic version, published for the first time by Maurice Heine in 1930 and recently republished by *Le Point du Jour*, arrived directly in the Bibliothèque Nationale. It seems to have been the loss of *Les Cent Vingt Journées de Sodome* which induced Sade to write a third, scandalous version of the story of Justine and to write the history of Juliette as a sequel. Having lost so essential a testimony, he must have wanted to substitute an equally complete work for it. It must also be said, however, that even this work lacks the monumental quality of *Les Cent Vingt Journées de Sodome*. We know that the curious manuscript of the latter book (a roll twelve metres long), which is supposed to have been found in Sade's cell by a certain Arnoux Saint-Maximin, was sold a century later by a French bookseller to a German collector. Dr. Dührer published it in Berlin in 1904, but gave a faulty version of it, printing 180 copies. Finally Maurice Heine, who brought it back to Paris in 1929, produced the standard text (Paris 1931-35) on which the 1947 and 1953 editions are based, though the publishers have corrected the spelling and omitted the errors carefully reproduced by Heine.

6. Quoted in Apollinaire, op. cit.
7. *La Nouvelle Justine*, t. III; quoted in Pierre Klossowski, *Sade, mon prochain*, Ed. du Seuil.
8. *Correspondance*. The letter does not bear the name of any recipient, but was no doubt addressed to Mlle Rousset, a pretty woman with whom Sade was briefly in love.
9. *La Philosophie dans le Boudoir*, 1795: 'Frenchmen, yet

another effort to be republicans... '

10. *Correspondance.*
11. In a letter to Gaufridy written before 15 July, 1775. (*Correspondance*).
12. Letter to Gaufridy, dated 5 January, 1791 (Op. cit., p. 301–302). Nor can anything be gathered from this passage in another letter to Gaufridy of 1776: 'There was no point in my complying with a man who started by insulting me, a fact which could later have set the very worst example, and above all on my land and in a country such as this where all vassals must show the respect which they owe and from which they are only too eager to escape at every moment.' (Op. cit.)
13. All that is certain is his deep-rooted hate for the clergy: 'The third is useless'.
14. *Les Infortunes de la Vertue*, Introduction.
15. *Sade, mon prochain.*
16. I do not share this reservation.
17. Published in 1931 (edited by Maurice Heine); Ed. Pauvert, 1953.
18. St. Benoist Labre is reputed to have gone as far as to eat his vermin. Klossowski ended his book with the words: 'If some great wit had asked St. Benoist Labre what he thought of his contemporary, the Marquis de Sade, the saint would have replied without hesitation: "He is my brother".'

PROUST

THE LOVE OF TRUTH AND JUSTICE AND MARCEL
PROUST'S SOCIALISM

The passion for truth and justice often gives those who
experience it a start. Those who experience it? But surely to
desire truth and justice is the same things as to be a man, to
be human. However unequally distributed such a passion
may be, it marks the extent to which each man is human –
to which human dignity is due to him. Marcel Proust wrote
in *Jean Santeuil*:

> It is always with a joyful and positive emotion that we
> hear those bold statements made by men of science
> who, for a mere question of professional honour, come
> to tell the truth – a truth which only interests them
> because it is true, and which they have to cherish in
> their art without hesitating to displease those who see
> it in a very different light and who regard it as part of a
> mass of considerations which interest them very
> little.[1]

The style and the content of this passage are very different
from *A la Recherche du temps perdu*. Yet, in the same book, the
style changes, but not the thought:

> What moves us so much in *Phaedo* is that, as we follow
> Socrates' arguments, we suddenly have the extra-
> ordinary feeling that we are listening to an argument
> whose purity is unaltered by any personal desire. We

feel as if truth were superior to everything, because we realise that the conclusion that Socrates is going to draw is that he must die.[2]

Marcel Proust wrote about the Dreyfus case around 1900. His *dreyfusard* sympathies are known to us all, but after *A la Recherche du temps perdu*, written ten years later, he lost his ingenuous aggressiveness. We ourselves have also lost that simplicity. The same passion may occasionally arouse us, but, on the whole, we are too tired, too indifferent. A Dreyfus case in our day would probably cause little stir. . . .

When we read *Jean Santeuil* we are amazed at the importance that politics had for Proust when he was thirty. Many readers will be astonished to see young Marcel boiling with rage because he was unable to applaud Jaurès' words in the Chamber of Deputies. In *Jean Santeuil* Jaurès appears under the name of Couzon. His black hair is curly but there is no room for doubt: he is 'the leader of the socialist party in the Chamber . . . the only great orator of our time, the equal of the greatest in antiquity.' Proust referred to 'the feeling of justice which sometimes seized him like a kind of inspiration'.[3] He depicted 'the odious imbeciles', the deputies of the majority, 'a sarcastic bunch who used their numerical superiority and the strength of their stupidity to attempt to drown the voice of Justice, which was ready to burst into song.'[4] Such sentiments are all the more surprising, coming as they do from a man whom one imagines to have been fairly indifferent to politics. The indifference into which he lapsed had several causes. There were, of course, his sexual obsessions. Then there was the fact that the bourgeoisie to which he belonged was threatened by the agitation of the working classes. Yet lucidity also played a part in the exhaustion of his youthful and revolutionary fervour.

Such fervour, we should bear in mind, was based on

sentiments completely alien to politics. It was 'hostility to his parents which aroused his unbounded enthusiasm for the actions of (Jaurès).'[5] This, admittedly, is Jean Santeuil speaking, but his character is that of Proust. We now know things that we would never have known had it not been for the publication of *Jean Santeuil*. We know that, in his youth, Proust had socialist sympathies, though he did, of course, have certain reservations. 'Whenever Jean really thought about it, he was amazed that (Jaurès) allowed his papers to print – indeed, that he himself was prepared to utter – such violent, almost slanderous, even cruel attacks against certain members of the majority.'[6] Though it is not the major obstacles in current politics which obstruct the truth, these obstacles had been known for some time. Proust's words might even be banal were they not impregnated with such gaucherie:

> Life, and above all politics, are surely a struggle, and since the wicked carry every weapon, it is the duty of the righteous to carry the same weapons, if only in order to rescue justice. We could almost say . . . that justice perishes because it is inadequately armed. But people will argue that if the great revolutionaries had looked at it too closely justice would never have triumphed.[7]

Proust was tormented by doubt from the start, and his preoccupations lacked consistency: he was no more than bothered by them. Yet, if he could forget them, it was only after he had fathomed their meaning and given his motives. In the fifth part of *Jean Santeuil* Jaurès, who would once 'have blushed at the mere idea of shaking a dishonest man by the hand',[8] who 'had constituted the very measure of justice for Jean' (the hero of the book), could not, when the time came, 'help crying when he thought of everything that he had sacrificed to his duty as party leader.'[9]

The plot of the book required Jaurès-Couzon to oppose a slanderous campaign against Jean's father. But, however great the author's affection for him, the politician could not 'alienate all those who had fought for him. He could not ruin his life's work and compromise the victory of his ideas in an attempt – a useless attempt because, were he to act alone, it was doomed to failure – to rehabilitate a moderate element who was wrongly suspected.' 'His passion for honesty, the difficulties he had encountered as he led it to victory, had forced him to identify his conduct with that of the strongest party to which he was obliged to sacrifice his personal preferences in exchange for the help which it gave him.'[10] Jean's voice, a voice from the past, from the time when the opposition still had some meaning, concludes with an ingenuousness which may now seem strange:

> You sacrifice the good of all not to a particular friendship, but to a particular interest – to your political situation. Yes, the good of all. Because when they are unjust towards my father, the journalists are not only being unjust. They make their readers unjust. They make them wicked. They make them want to say that one of their neighbours, whom they thought was good, is wicked . . . I believe that they will triumph one day, and that this triumph will be the triumph of Injustice. As they await the day when the government becomes unjust and injustice will really exist, they make calumny and the love of scandal and cruelty reign in every heart.[11]

MORALITY IN CONNECTION WITH TRANSGRESSION OF THE MORAL LAW

So ingenuous a tone is surprising in so disingenuous a writer. But can we let ourselves be taken in by what, for a moment, seems to have been his innermost conviction? All we are really left with is the admission of a first instinct. Nobody will be surprised to read these words in the third volume of *Jean Santeuil*: '... how often do we write that "There is only one truly base thing which dishonours the creature which God has created in His image – lying."? This means that what we really want to avoid is being lied to. It does not mean that we really believe it.' Proust then added:

> Jean did not admit (to his mistress) that he had seen the letter through the envelope, and since he could not help telling her that a young man had come to visit her, he said that he had heard it from somebody who had seen her – a lie. But this did not prevent his eyes from filling with tears when he told her that the only truly atrocious thing was a lie.[12]

Carried away by jealousy, the man who had accused Jaurès became a cynic.

Nevertheless this youthful and ingenuous honesty is an interesting phenomenon. In *A la Recherche du temps perdu* the evidence of Marcel's cynicism accumulates when jealousy drives him to tortuous manoeuvres. But these very different forms of behaviour, which initially seem to exclude each other, merge. If we had no scruples, if we did not care to observe rigid taboos, we would not be human beings. But we are unable to observe these taboos for ever – if we did not occasionally have the courage to break them, we would find ourselves in a cul-de-sac. It is also true that we would not be human if we never had, if we had not once had, the heart to be unjust. We ridicule the contradiction between war and the universal taboo which condemns murder, but war, like the taboo, is universal. Murder is always laden with horror, while acts of war are always considered valorous. The same applies to lies and injustice. In certain places taboos have indeed been rigorously observed, but the timid man, who never dares break the law, who turns away, is everywhere despised. The idea of virility always contains the image of the man who, within his limitations, can put himself above the law deliberately, fearlessly and thoughtlessly. Had Jaurès yielded to justice he would not only have injured his supporters: his supporters would have considered him hopelessly incompetent. Virility has a deaf side which commands us never to provide an answer or offer an explanation. We must be loyal, scrupulous and disinterested, but beyond these scruples, this loyalty and this disinterestedness, we must be sovereign.

The necessity of at one point violating the taboo, even if it be sacred, does not invalidate the principle. The man who lied and, as he lied, claimed that 'the only truly atrocious thing was a lie' loved truth until he died. Emmanuel Berl has given us a description of the effect Proust's integrity had on him:

One night, after I had left Proust's house at about three in the morning (it was during the war), I found myself alone in the boulevard Haussmann, bewildered and harassed by a conversation which had exhausted both my physical and intellectual resources. I felt that I was at the end of my tether. I was almost as bewildered as I had been when my shelter in Bois-le-Prêtre collapsed. I could no longer bear anything, starting with myself. I was exhausted and ashamed of my exhaustion. I thought about this man who hardly ate, who was stifled by asthma and was unable to sleep, but at the same time fought against lies as unhesitatingly as he fought against death. He did not stop before analysis or the difficulty of formulating the results of analysis. He was even prepared to make the additional effort to sort out the cowardly confusion of

> my own ideas. I was less disgusted by my confusion
> than by my listlessness in putting up with it...

Such avidity is by no means contrary to the transgression of a point within its own principle. It is too great for the principle to be threatened – even hesitation would be a weakness. At the basis of every virtue is our power to break its hold. Traditional education has neglected this secret resource of morality, and the idea of morality is enfeebled by it. If we place ourselves on the side of virtue moral life appears like a timorous conformism. If we stand on the other side, contempt for insipidity is considered immoral. Traditional education seeks in vain for a surface discipline composed of logical formalism: it turns its back on the spirit of discipline. When Nietzsche denounced traditional morality he thought he would never survive a crime he might have committed. If there is an authentic morality, its existence is always at stake. True hatred of lying acknowledges, after overcoming its disgust, the risk contained in telling a lie. Indifference to risk is due to its apparent lightness. It is the reverse of eroticism which acknowledges the condemnation without which it would be insipid. The concept of intangible laws removes some of its power from a moral truth to which we should adhere, but without tying ourselves down to it. In erotic excess we venerate the rule which we break. A series of rebounding oppositions lies at the basis of an instinct composed alternately of fidelity and revolt, which is the essence of man. Outside this series we are stifled by the logic of laws.

PLEASURE BASED ON THE CRIMINAL SENSE OF EROTICISM

By relating his experience of erotic life, Proust has provided us with an intelligible aspect of this fascinating series of oppositions. One scholar[13] has spotted, in a somewhat arbitrary manner, the symptoms of a pathological state in the association between murder and sacrilege and the absolutely holy image of the mother. 'While pleasure held me more and more firmly in its grip,' writes the narrator of *A la Recherche du temps perdu*, 'I felt infinite sadness and desolation aroused in the depths of my heart; I thought I made my mother's soul weep...' Sensual pleasure depended on this feeling of horror. At one point in *A la Recherche du temps perdu* Marcel's mother disappears, though no mention is made of her death: only his grandmother's death is reported. As if his mother's death meant too much for him, Marcel writes of his grandmother: 'Comparing my grandmother's death to that of Albertine, I thought that my life was branded by a double murder.'

To the stigma of assassination was added another, still deeper stigma: that of profanation. Let us examine the passage in *Sodome et Gomorrhe* where 'the sons, not always resembling their father, fulfil the profanation of their mother in their faces'. The author concludes: 'Let us abandon at this point a topic which deserves a chapter to itself'. Indeed, the key to this particular tragedy is the episode when Vinteuil's daughter, whose father had died from grief at her behaviour, made love, in her mourning clothes, a few days after the funeral, with a Lesbian who spat on the dead man's photograph. Vinteuil's daughter personifies Marcel, and Vinteuil is Marcel's mother.[14] Mademoiselle Vinteuil's invitation to her lover to stay while her father was still alive is a parallel to the narrator's inviting Albertine (in real life the chauffeur Albert Agostinelli) to stay in his apartment. Nothing is said about the mother's reaction to the guest. I imagine that no reader can fail to have noticed that in this the story is imperfect. Vinteuil's death, on the other hand, is recounted in detail. The blank spaces left by Proust are filled in by the passages concerning Vinteuil, which prove so distressing to read if we alter the names.

For those who, like ourselves, saw [Marcel's mother] avoiding [her] acquaintances, turning away when [she] saw them, aged in a few months, consumed by misery, becoming incapable of any effort which was not aimed directly at [her son's] happiness, spending entire days before [her husband's] tomb, it would be hard not to realise that [she] was dying of misery and to suppose that [she] was unaware of the rumours in circulation. [She] knew about them: [she] may even have confirmed them. There is surely not one person, however virtuous, whom the complexity of circumstances cannot one day oblige to live in familiarity with the vice he condemns most outrightly, without his recognising it fully beneath the disguise of the particular facts which it dons in order to enter into contact with him and make him suffer: bizarre words, inexplicable attitudes, on a certain evening, of a certain person whom he has so many reasons to love. But [a woman] like [Marcel's mother] suffered more than most people when she resigned herself to one of those situations which we mistakenly regard as the exclusive prerogatives of the Bohemian world: they occur every time a vice, nurtured by nature herself in a child, requires the place and security necessary for its indulgence... But the fact that [Marcel's mother] may have known about [her son's] behaviour by no means diminished [her] adoration of [him]. Facts do not penetrate the world of our beliefs; they do not give birth to them, any more than they destroy them...

We can also attribute to Marcel that which is attributed, in *A la Recherche du temps perdu*, to Mademoiselle Vinteuil:

In [Marcel's] heart evil, to start with, at least, was not undiluted. A sadist like [Marcel] is the artist of evil in a way that an entirely evil creature could never be, for evil would never be outside him; it would seem quite natural to him; it would never even be clear to him; and since [he] would have no part in virtue, respect for the dead, or filial affection, [he] would have no sacrilegious pleasure in desecrating them. Sadists of [Marcel's] kind are purely sentimental beings, so naturally virtuous that even sensual pleasure seems bad to them – the privilege of the wicked. And when they allow themselves to yield to it for an instant, they try to enter the wicked man's skin and drag their accomplice into it, so as, in one moment, to have the illusion of having escaped from their scrupulous and tender soul into the inhuman world of pleasure.

Proust also added in *Le Temps retrouvé*: 'In the sadist – however good he may be, indeed, the better he is the more it exists – there is a thirst for evil which the wicked, acting for other ends (if they are wicked for some admissible reason), can never satisfy.' Just as disgust is the measure of love, thirst for Evil is the measure of Good.

The clarity of this picture is fascinating. What is disturbing in it is the possibility of grasping one aspect without its complementary aspect. Evil seems to be understandable, but only to the extent in which Good is the key to it. If the luminous intensity of Good did not give the night of Evil its blackness, Evil would lose its appeal. This is a difficult point to understand. Something flinches in him who faces up to it. And yet we know that the strongest effects on the senses are caused by contrasts. The movement of sensual life is based on the fear which the male inspires in the female, and on the brutal agony of copulation – it is less a harmony than a violence which may lead to harmony, but through excess. In the first place it is necessary to effect a break – union comes at the end of a tournament at which death is the stake. An agonising aspect of love emerges from its multiple experiences. If love is sometimes pink, pink goes well with black, without which it would be a sign of insipidity. Without black, pink would surely lose that quality which affects the senses. Without misfortune, bound to it as shade is to light, indifference would correspond to happiness. Novels describe suffering, hardly ever satisfaction. The virtue of happiness is ultimately its rarity. Were it easily accessible it would be despised and associated with boredom. The transgression of the rule alone has that irresistible attraction which lasting happiness lacks.

The most powerful scene in *A la Recherche du temps perdu* (which puts it on a level with the blackest tragedy) would not have the profound significance we attribute to it if this first aspect were not counterbalanced. If pink has to be contrasted with black in order to suggest desire, would this black be black enough had we never thirsted for purity? had it not tarnished our dream *in spite of ourselves*? Impurity is only known by contrast by those who thought they could not do without its opposite, purity. The absolute desire for impurity, artificially conceived by Sade, led him to that sated state in which every blunted sensation, even the possibility of pleasure, ultimately escaped him. Not even the infinite resource offered him by literature (the imaginary scenes of his novels) could satisfy him. He never knew the particular delight of the moral feeling that gives our sins that criminal flavour without which they seem natural, without which *they are natural*.

Proust was more able than Sade. Eager to have his pleasure, he left vice the odious colour of vice - the condemnation of virtue. But if he was virtuous, it was not in order to obtain pleasure, and if he obtained pleasure it was because he had first wanted to obtain virtue. The wicked only know the material benefits of Evil. If they seek other people's misfortune, this misfortune is ultimately their selfish fortune. We only escape the imbroglio where Evil lies concealed by perceiving the interdependence of opposites. To start with I showed that happiness alone is not desirable in itself and would result in boredom if the experience of misfortune, or of Evil, did not make us long for it. The opposite is also true: had we not, like Proust (and, maybe, even Sade), longed for Good, Evil would provide us with a succession of indifferent sensations.

JUSTICE, TRUTH AND PASSION

What emerges from this is the rectification of the common view which inattentively sees Good in opposition to Evil. Though Good and Evil are complementary, there is no equivalence. We are right to distinguish between behaviour which has a *humane* sense and behaviour which has an odious sense. But the opposition between these forms of behaviour is not that which theoretically opposes Good to Evil.

The poverty of tradition is to rest on that feebleness which determines the care of the future. Care of the future is the exaltation of avarice; it condemns improvidence, which squanders. Provident weakness opposes the principle of enjoying the present moment. Traditionally morality complies with avarice: it sees the roots of Evil in the preference for immediate pleasure. Avaricious morality is at the basis of justice and the police. If I like pleasure, I deplore repression. The paradox of justice is that avaricious morality ties it to the narrowness of repression, while generous morality sees it as the primary impulse of him who wants every man to have his due, who runs to the assistance of the victim of injustice. Could justice survive without this generosity? and who could say that it was 'ready to burst into song'?

Would truth be what it is if it did not assert itself

generously against falsehood? The passion for truth and justice is often far removed from the political masses, for the masses, which are sometimes stimulated by generosity, are sometimes moved by the opposite tendency. In ourselves generosity is always contrasted with avarice, just as passion is contrasted with calculation. We cannot yield blindly to a passion which also involves avarice; but generosity transcends reason and is always passionate. There is something passionate, generous and sacred in us which exceeds the representations of the mind: it is this excess which makes us human. It would be fruitless to talk of justice and truth in a world of intelligent automats.

It was only because he expected something sacred from it that truth aroused the sort of anger in Marcel Proust which terrified Emmanuel Berl. Berl has left us a description of the scene when Proust threw him out of his house, shouting: 'Get out! Get out!' Berl had planned to marry and Proust decided that he was lost to his truth. Was this folly? Perhaps, but would truth confer itself on someone who did not love it to the point of folly? I repeat Berl's words:

> His pale face turned still paler. His eyes sparkled with rage. He got to his feet and went into his dressing room to change. He had to go out. I was aware of his energy. Hitherto I had paid little attention to it. His hair was darker and thicker than mine, his teeth healthier, and his heavy jaw seemed exceptionally mobile. His chest, swollen with asthma no doubt, emphasised the breadth of his shoulders.[15] If we were to come to blows, as I thought for a second we might, I was not sure of being able to hold my own.

Truth – and justice – require calm, and yet they only belong to the violent.

Though our moments of passion remove us from the

coarser requisites of political combat, it is as well to keep in mind that the masses can sometimes be moved by a generous wrath. This is surprising but significant: Proust himself emphasised the irreconcilable element which exists between the police and the generosity of the masses. Proust, who worshipped truth, described the passion for justice which once seized him. He imagined himself, under its impact, 'furiously returning the blows which the weaker man was receiving. Similarly, on the day he heard that a thief had been denounced, surrounded and then, after a desperate resistance, garotted by the police, he had wished that he had been strong enough to murder the policemen.'[16]

I was moved by this rebellious instinct, so unexpected in Proust. I see it as the association between anger, stifled by prolonged reflection, and wisdom, without which anger is pointless. If the obscurity of wrath and the lucidity of wisdom do not ultimately coincide, how can we recognise ourselves in this world? But the fragments are to be found on the peak – it is there that we grasp the truth, which is composed of opposites, Good and Evil.

NOTES

1. Marcel Proust, *Jean Santeuil*, Gallimard, 1952.
2. Ibid.
3. Ibid.
4. Ibid.
5. Ibid.
6. Ibid.
7. Ibid.
8. Ibid.
9. Ibid.
10. Ibid.
11. Ibid.
12. Ibid.
13. André Fretet, *L'Aliénation poétique. Rimbaud, Mallarmé, Proust*, Janin, 1946.
14. Marie-Anne Cochet and Henri Massis have long proposed this identification, which can now be considered definite.
15. One of the most recent photographs of Marcel Proust corresponds to this disconcerting description of him. See Georges Cattaui, *Marcel Proust*, Julliard, 1952.
16. Marcel Proust, *Jean Santeuil*.

KAFKA

SHOULD KAFKA BE BURNT?

Soon after the War a Communist weekly paper, *Action*, opened an inquiry into an unexpected subject. *Should Kafka be burnt?* the editors asked. The question was all the more incongruous since it was not preceded by anything which might have led into it: should books be burnt? Or, what sort of book should be burnt? However that may be, the editors' choice was subtle. The author of *The Trial* is, as they say, 'one of the greatest geniuses of our time'. Nevertheless the large number of replies proved that boldness paid. Besides, even before it had been formulated, the inquiry had received an answer which the editors omitted to publish – Kafka's own answer. For he lived, or at any rate died, tormented by the desire to burn his books.

To my mind Kafka remained undecided until the end. To start with, he wrote his books, and we must imagine a period of time between the day when one writes something and the day when one decides to burn what one has written. Then his decision remained equivocal: he conferred the task of burning his work on his one friend who had already informed him that he would never do so. Yet, before his death, he did indeed express a decisive wish that all he left should be thrown into the fire.

In all events the idea of burning Kafka, even it if was no more than a provocation, had a certain logic for the

Communists. Those imaginary flames contribute to the understanding of his books. They are books doomed to the flames: they are there, but they are there in order to disappear, as though they have already been annihilated.

KAFKA, THE PROMISED LAND AND REVOLUTIONARY SOCIETY

Of all writers Kafka was possibly the most cunning: he, at least, was never had! To start with, unlike many modern writers, he wanted to be a writer. He realised that literature, which was what he wanted, denied him the satisfaction he expected, but he never stopped writing. We cannot even say that literature disappointed him. It did not disappoint him – not, at any rate, in comparison with other possible goals. For him, literature was what the promised land was for Moses. 'The fact that he was not to see the Promised Land until just before his death is incredible,' Kafka wrote about Moses in his diary. 'The sole significance of this last view is to show how imperfect an instant human life is – imperfect, because this aspect of life (the expectation of the Promised Land) could last indefinitely without ever appearing to be more than an instant. Moses did not fail to reach Canaan because his life was too short, but because his was a human life.'[1] This is no longer a mere denunciation of the vanity of one 'aspect of life', but of the vanity of all endeavours, which are equally senseless: an endeavour is always as hopeless in time as a fish in water. It is a mere point in the movement of the universe, *for we are dealing with a human life.*

Is anything more contrary to the position of the Communists? Communism is action *par excellence*, action which changes the world. In Communism the goal, the altered world, situated in time, in the future, takes precedence over existence, or present activity, which is only significant in as far as it leads towards the goal: *the world must change.* Communism, therefore, raises no problem of principle. The whole of humanity is prepared to subordinate the present moment to the imperative power of a goal. Nobody doubts the value or questions the ultimate authority of action.

All that remains is an insignificant reservation: we tell ourselves that action has never prevented anyone from living . . . Thus the world of action never has any care other than its goal. The goals differ according to the intention, but their diversity, even their opposition, has always held a place for individual convenience. Only a deformed, almost insane man refuses one goal in favour of anything other than a still more valid goal. Kafka himself implies that Moses was only an object of derision because he had to die in accordance with the prophecy as soon as he reached his goal. But he adds, logically, that the underlying cause of his defeat was his 'human life'. The aim is postponed in time and time is limited: this alone leads Kafka to regard the goal in itself as a lure.

This is so paradoxical – and so totally opposed to the Communist mentality (and not merely to the political belief that nothing counts except the revolution) – that we must examine Kafka's attitude a little more closely.

KAFKA'S PERFECT PUERILITY

The task is by no means easy. Whenever Kafka decided to express his ideas (in his diary or in his various notes), he made a trap of every word. He constructed perilous edifices in which the words had no logical order but were simply piled on top of each other as if they were only there to astonish and disorientate, as if they were addressed to the author himself who never seemed to tire of proceeding from astonishment to bewilderment.

What we cannot do is to attribute a meaning to Kafka's truly literary writings. We frequently see something that is not there, or, at best, we see something that is there but at which we can no more than hint.[2] Nevertheless we can follow a general direction in this labyrinth which only becomes clear to us when we find our way out of it. At that point I think we can simply say that Kafka's work reveals a totally childish attitude.

In my opinion the weakness of the world we live in is to consider childishness a sphere apart which, though not alien to us, remains outside us and which is incapable of representing its truth – what it really is – on its own. Equally, nobody regards error as representing truth. 'It's childish' or 'it's not serious' are equivalent propositions. Yet we are all childish – totally, unreservedly, and, we should even add, in the most surprising way. It is thus (by childishness) that humanity, in its nascent state, shows its essential nature. In a way an animal is never childish, but the young human being connects – sometimes even passionately – the senses suggested to him by the adult to some other sense which he cannot connect with anything. Such is the world to which we adhered and which once intoxicated us with its innocence – a world where each thing temporarily rejected that which made it a thing within the adult system.

Kafka left what his publisher called the 'outline of an autobiography'.[3] The fragment refers solely to his child-hood and to one particular trait. 'You will find it impossible to persuade a boy engrossed in a fascinating story that he must go to bed, if you try to do so by proving that it is for his own good.' Further on Kafka says: 'The most important thing about all this is that I extended the condemnation which my exaggerated amount of reading had earned for me to a secret failure to perform my duty, and therefore arrived at the most depressing conclusions.'

The adult author insists on the fact that the condemnation was directed against tastes which constituted the 'child's particularities'. Constraint either made him 'hate the oppressor' or consider insignificant the peculiarities which he defended. 'If I concealed one of my peculiarities,' he wrote, 'I ended up by hating myself or my destiny, and considered myself wicked or accursed.'

The reader of *The Trial* or *The Castle* will have no difficulty in recognising the atmosphere of Kafka's romantic compositions. When he was older, the crime of reading was succeeded by the crime of writing. When it came to literature, the people surrounding Kafka, above all his father, were no less disapproving than they had been when they had caught him reading. And Kafka was equally desperate. As Michel Carrouges rightly said: 'What he resented so terribly was the levity with which his deepest preoccupations were considered . . . ' Describing a scene when his family's contempt became cruelly obvious, Kafka wrote: 'I remained seated and leaned towards my family as I had done before, but in fact I had been banished from society with one stroke.'[4]

THE SUSTENANCE OF THE INFANTILE SITUATION

The odd thing about Kafka is that he wanted his father to understand him and to comply with the childishness of what he read and, later, of what he wrote. He did not want his father to banish from adult society, which alone was indestructible, the very thing which, since infancy, he had identified as the essential characteristic of himself. For him, his father was the figure of authority whose interest was limited to the values of effective action. His father symbolised the primacy of a goal, subordinating present life, which most adults respected. Like every true writer,

Kafka lived childishly under the primacy of his goal, as opposed to present desire. Admittedly he subjected himself to the torture of an office job, though not without complaining about his ill-fortune, if not about the people who compelled him to work. He always felt excluded from the society which employed him, but he considered worthless – childish – that very thing that was, basically, himself. His father obviously replied with the incomprehension of the world of action.

In 1919 Franz Kafka wrote his father a letter[5] which, fortunately, no doubt, he never posted and of which we only possess certain fragments. He said:

> I was a frightened child, but, like all children, I was obstinate. Undoubtedly my mother spoiled me, and yet I cannot believe that I was quite unmanageable, that a kind word, a pat on my hand, a kind look, would not have obtained all you wanted from me. You can only treat a child in accordance with your true nature, that is to say with force and violence... You rose to such a high position on your own, through your own strength, because you had unlimited faith in your opinions... In your presence I started stammering... When I stood before you I lost all self-confidence and assumed, instead, an unbounded sense of guilt. It was with this unbounded sense of guilt in mind that I once wrote of somebody[6] 'He feared that the shame would outlive him...' Whenever I wrote anything it was about you. What do I do but pour out the groans and laments which I was unable to release before you? Everything has been a leave-taking from you, voluntarily protracted.

Kafka wanted to entitle his entire work 'Attempts to escape from the paternal sphere'.[7] Yet let there be no mistake about it: Kafka never really wanted to escape. What he really wanted was to live within the paternal sphere – *as an exile*. Basically he knew that he had been banished. We cannot tell whether he was banished by others or by himself. He simply behaved in such a manner as to be odious to the world of industrial and commercial interest: he wanted to remain within the puerility of a dream.

The escape he dreamt of differed essentially from the traditional form of literary escapism in that it failed – it had to fail and it wanted to fail. What common escape lacks – and by lacking it is limited to a compromise, to a 'sham' – is the profound sense of guilt, of the violation of an indestructible law, the lucidity of a pitiless self-knowledge. The man who escapes in literature is a dilettante who knows that he is amusing himself. He is not yet free – he is not free in the true sense of the word, where liberty is sovereign. To be free, he would have to be recognised as such by the dominant society.

In the old-fashioned world of Austrian feudalism, the only society that could have recognised the young Israelite for reasons other than literary snobbery, was his father's business world. The world in which the power of Franz's father was incontestably affirmed, stood for the hard competition of work which yielded nothing to caprice and which, though it tolerated, and even loved childishness within certain limits, condemned childishness on principle, and confined it to childhood. This brings us to Kafka's extremism. He wanted to be recognised by the authority least likely to recognise him and to which he was determined never to yield. At the same time, however, he never intended to overthrow this authority or even to oppose it. He did not want to oppose the father who had even taken the possibility of living from him. He, in his turn, never wanted to be an adult or a father. In his own way he struggled all his life, and with full exercise of all his rights to enter his father's society, but he would only have accepted admission on one condition – *that of remaining the irresponsible child he was.*

He pursued this desperate struggle relentlessly. He never had any hope: his only way out was to enter his father's world through death, thereby abandoning all his peculiarities, his whims and his childishness. He himself formulated this solution – constantly repeated in his novels – in 1917: 'I will confide in death,' he said. 'The remains of a belief. *Return to the father.* Great day of reconciliation.'[8] The only way for him to become a father was by marrying, but he avoided this despite the excellent reasons he had for wanting to marry: he broke off his engagement twice. He lived 'isolated from past generations' and 'he never managed to head a generation himself.'[9]

'The main obstacle to my marriage,' he wrote in his letter to his father, 'is my definitive conviction that, in order to insure the existence of a family, and, above all, in order to direct it, one needs the qualities which I know you possess...'[10] One must, in other words, be what you are and betray what I am.

Kafka could choose between the puerile but discreet scandals of caprice and sovereign humour. These, heeding nothing, subordinate nothing to a promised happiness, and the quest for this happiness, which is due as a reward for laborious activity and manly authority. He had the choice: he proved it. He knew, if not how to deny himself and lose himself in the mechanism of a thankless job, how to perform it conscientiously. He chose the unrestrained caprice of his heroes, their childishness and carelessness, their scandalous behaviour and obvious lies. In a word, he wanted an irrational world, which escaped classification, to remain supreme and to provide an existence only possible to the extent in which it called for death.

He desired this irrevocably and uncompromisingly, refusing to leave the sovereign value of his choice any chance of disguise. He never deviated by requesting the privilege of seriousness for something which has no right to be sovereign. What are whims guaranteed by law and authority other than wild animals in the zoo? He felt that truth, the authenticity of caprice, required illness and turmoil. Prerogatives, as Maurice Blanchot said of him,[11] pertain to action, 'art (caprice) has no prerogatives against action'. The world is necessarily the property of those to whom a promised land has been attributed and who, if needs be, join forces and struggle in order to obtain it. Kafka's silent and desperate strength was never to want to question the authority which denied him the possibility of living and to avoid the common error of competing under the pressure of authority.

If he wins, the man who once rejected constraint becomes, for himself as well as for others, like those whom he once fought against and who constrained him. Puerility, sovereign, uncalculating caprice, cannot survive their victory. Sovereignty can only exist on the condition that it should never assume power, which is action, the primacy of the future over the present moment, the primacy of the promised land. It is hard not to struggle in order to destroy a cruel adversary. It is to offer oneself to death. To survive without betraying oneself requires a relentless, austere, agonising struggle: this is the only chance of maintaining that delirious purity which is never tied to logic and can never fit in to the mechanism of action – that purity which drags all its heroes into the mire of a growing guilt. Is anyone more childish or more silently incongruous than K. in *The Castle* or than Joseph K. in *The Trial*? This double character, 'the same in both books, sullenly aggressive, irrationally, uncalculatingly aggressive, is lost by a whim, by the obstinacy of a blind man. He expects everything from the benevolence of pitiless authorities. He behaves like the boldest libertine in the public room of an inn (and, what is worse, of the inn of the authorities), in the middle of a school, in the presence of his lawyer . . . in the High Court of Justice'.[12]

The father in *The Verdict* is turned to scorn by the son, but he is always sure that the deep, exhaustive, fatal, involuntary destruction of his authority will be punished. The man who introduces disorder has unleashed his hounds without finding a hiding place. He himself will be their first victim, torn to pieces in the dark. This, no doubt, is the doom of all that is humanly sovereign. Sovereignty survives either by denying itself (even the smallest calculation is on the ground level: only subservience remains, the primacy of the object of calculation over the present), or else in the durable moment of Death. Death is the only means of avoiding the abdication of sovereignty. There is no subservience in death; in death there is nothing.

FRANZ KAFKA'S JOYOUS UNIVERSE

Kafka does not evoke sovereign life: on the contrary, the life he evokes, contorted even in its most capricious moments, is unremittingly sad. The eroticism in *The Trial* and *The Castle* is an eroticism without love, desire or strength, an arid eroticism from which one should escape at all costs. But everything becomes confused. In 1922[13] Kafka noted in his diary:

> Whenever I was satisfied I wanted to be unsatisfied and sought dissatisfaction by all the means of time and tradition accessible to me: then I wanted to turn back. So I was always unsatisfied, even by my dissatisfaction. It is odd that with enough systematisation some reality should have come out of this ridiculous situation. My mental decline started as a

childish game, though admittedly it was a consciously childish game. For example, I pretended to have nervous tics. I went around with my arms crossed behind my head, a detestably childish thing to do, but it was successful. The same went for the development of my writing, a development which later unfortunately came to a halt. If it is possible to produce misery one should produce it thus.

But elsewhere we find an undated fragment:[14] 'I do not hope for victory, I do not enjoy the struggle for its own sake, I could only enjoy it because it is all I can do. As such the struggle does indeed fill me with a joy which is more than I can really enjoy, more than I can give, and I shall probably end by succumbing not to the struggle but to the joy.'

He wanted to be miserable for his own satisfaction: the most secret part of this misery was such an intense form of joy that he spoke of dying of it. 'He leaned his head to one side, revealing his throat where a wound bubbled in the burning flesh and blood, caused by a lightning flash, which still lasts.'[15] The blinding flash – the lasting flash – doubtless has a greater significance than the depression which preceded it. We find the following remarkable passage in Kafka's diary in 1917:[16]

I could never understand that it was possible for almost anyone who could write to objectivise pain in pain. For example, in my misery, with my head still burning with misery, I can sit down and write to somebody: I am miserable. I can go still further and, in various flourishes, according to my capacities, which seem to have nothing in common with my misery, I can improvise on this theme, simply, antithetically, or even with entire orchestras of associations. And that is no lie; it does not alleviate the pain: it is an excess of strength accorded by grace in a moment when pain has visibly exhausted all my energy, to the very depths of my being, which it continues to flay. What is this excess?

Let us take up this question: what is this excess? Of all Kafka's stories few are as interesting as *The Verdict*. We read in his diary on September 23, 1912,[17]

> This story was written in one stretch on the night of the 22nd to the 23rd, from ten at night to six in the morning. I could hardly withdraw my legs from under the table, so stiff had they grown. The terrible effort and joy of seeing the story develop before me – how I made my way through the waters. Several times, during the course of the night, I bore all my weight on my back. How everything can be said; how, for every idea that comes to mind, even for the strangest ideas, a great fire waits for them to disappear and resurrect.

Carrouges says:[18]

> This new tale is the story of a young man who quarrels with his father about the existence of a friend and ends by committing suicide. In a few lines, as short as the description of the quarrel is long, we are told how the young man kills himself:
>
>> He rushed out of the door and crossed the tram lines, pulled irresistibly towards the water. He clung to the parapet as a starving man clings to his food. He jumped over the safety rail, like the expert gymnast he had been in his youth, his parents' pride. He held himself for another instant with a weakening grip, watched a bus pass between the bars, the roar it made would easily drown the sound of his fall, he cried feebly:

'Dear parents, I have always loved you', and let himself go. At that moment the traffic on the bridge was literally frantic.

Michel Carrouges is right to insist on the poetic value of this last phrase. Kafka himself gave another interpretation to the pious Max Brod: 'Do you know,' he asked, 'what the last phrase means? As I wrote it I thought of a violent ejaculation.'[19] Does this 'extraordinary declaration' give us a glimpse of an 'erotic basis'? Does it mean that 'in the act of writing there is a sort of compensation for the defeat before the father and the failure of the dream of transmitting life?'[20] I do not know, but in the light of this 'declaration' the phrase expresses the sovereignty of joy, the supreme lapse of being into that nothingness which the others constitute for the being.

The mere fact of dying compensates for this sovereignty of joy.[21] Anguish preceded it, like an awareness of the fatality of the issue, as though it were already apprehension of the moment of intoxication, which the condemnation of the delivering vertigo – or death – will be. But misery is not exclusively punishment. The death of George Bendemann had for Kafka, his double, a sense of happiness: voluntary condemnation prolonged the excess which had provoked it, but removed the anguish by according the father a definite love, a definite respect. There was no other way of reconciling profound veneration with deliberate lack of veneration. This is the price of sovereignty: its only right is death: it can never act, never demand the prerogatives which pertain to action alone, to that action which is never authentically sovereign because of that servile quality inherent in any search for results, to that action which is always subordinate. Is there anything unexpected in this complicity between death and pleasure? Pleasure – that which pleases uncalculatingly, in spite of calculation –

being the attribute or the emblem of the sovereign being, it has death as its penalty, as well as having it as its means.

That is all there is to say. Lightning or joy are not produced in moments of eroticism. If eroticism is there, it is to ensure disorder, like the feigned nervous tics with which Kafka wanted to 'produce misery'. Only increased misfortune and a totally indefensible way of life bring about the necessity of struggle and this anguish which grips us by the throat, without which neither the excess nor the grace would exist. Misery and sin already constitute a struggle in themselves. The struggle, whose innermost sense is virtue, is not dependent on results. If it lacked anguish, the struggle would not be 'all he could do'. Only when he is in misery, therefore, is Kafka filled 'with a joy which is more than [he] can really enjoy, more than [he] can give.' Then the joy is so intense that it is from the joy and not from the struggle that he expects death.

THE CHILD'S HAPPY EXUBERANCE IS RECOVERED IN DEATH'S EXPRESSION OF SOVEREIGN LIBERTY

One of Kafka's pieces, *Kinder auf der Landstrasse*, shows a paradoxical aspect of his happy exuberance. As in all the other moments described in his work, nothing here is solidly attached to the established order or to definable relationships. There is always that same formless laceration, sometimes slow and sometimes fast, of mist in the wind. Never does a clear goal, openly aimed at, give a significance to the absence of limit which so passively reigns sovereign. As a child Kafka joined a group of playmates:

> Our heads down, we ran through the evening. Daytime, nighttime, they no longer existed. Our waistcoat buttons knocked together like teeth, we ran

one after the other, our mouths on fire, like tropical animals. Prancing and rearing, like the cuirassiers of ancient wars, we drove each other down the short lane and way up the high road. Isolated figures leapt into the ditch, but hardly had they disappeared in the darkness of the embankment than they reappeared up on the path by the edge of the fields, looking down on us like strangers . . .

This 'contrary' (just as the sun is the contrary of the impenetrable mists, of which it is also the veiled truth) may help us to understand Kafka's seemingly sad work. The overwhelming impetus of his childhood, crying with joy, later became absorbed by death. Death alone was vast enough, sufficiently well hidden from the 'action-pursuing-the-goal' to excite covertly Kafka's devlish humour. In other words, in the acceptance of death, within the limitations of death, subordinated to the goal, Kafka found that sovereign attitude which aims at nothing, wants nothing, resumes, in a flash, its fullness and its wildness. When Bendemann jumped over the parapet, the impetus was that of vagabond childhood. The sovereign attitude is guilty, miserable in so far as it tries to flee from death, but, just as it dies, the wild feeling of childhood is again suffused with useless liberty. The living, which was irreducible, refused what death accords. Death alone yields to the full authority of action, but it does not suffer from it.

JUSTIFICATION OF COMMUNIST HOSTILITY

In Kafka's work we can distinguish a social aspect, a familial and sexual aspect, and finally a religious aspect. But such distinctions seem slightly superfluous to me: I have hitherto attempted to introduce a point of view in which all these aspects are combined. The social character of Kafka's stories can no doubt only be grasped in a general context. To see the 'epic of the unemployed' or of 'the persecuted Jew' in *The Castle*, the 'epic of the defendant in the bureaucratic era' in *The Trial*; to compare these obsessive tales with Rousset's *Univers concentrationnaire*, is not entirely justifiable. But this brings Carrouges, who does so, to an analysis of Communist hostility. It would have been easy, he tells us, 'to defend Kafka from every charge of being a counter-revolutionary if one had wanted to say of him, as of others, that he limited himself to depicting the capitalist hell.'[22] 'If Kafka's attitude seems odious to so many revolutionaries,' he adds, 'it is not because it explicitly attacks bourgeois bureaucracy and justice – an attack with which they would have concurred – but because it attacks every type of bureaucracy and pseudo-justice.'[23] Did Kafka want to criticise certain institutions for which we should have substituted other, less inhuman ones? Carrouges writes again: 'Does he advise against revolt? No more than he encourages it. He merely affirms man's collapse: the reader can draw his own conclusions. And how can one not rebel against the odious power which prevents the land-surveyor from working?' I believe, on the other hand, that the very idea of revolt is deliberately withdrawn from *The Castle*. Carrouges knows this, and says a little further on:[24] 'The only criciticism one can level at Kafka is the scepticism with which he regards every revolutionary undertaking, for he sets problems which are not political problems, but which are human and eternally post-revolutionary problems.' But to talk of scepticism and to give Kafka's problems a significance with regard to the words and actions of political humanity, is not going far enough.

Far from being incongruous, Communist hostility is essentially connected with an understanding of Kafka. I shall go still further. Kafka's attitude towards his father's

authority symbolises hostility towards the general authority which stems from *effective activity*. Effective activity,
elevated to the discipline of as rational a system as that of
Communists, is apparently presented as the solution to
every problem. Yet it can neither totally condemn, nor
tolerate, in practice, a truly sovereign attitude in which the
present moment is detached from those that follow. This is
a difficulty for a party which respects reason alone and
which sees those irrational values where luxury, uselessness
and childishness occur, as masks on the face of private
interest. The only sovereign attitude permitted by the
Communists is that of the child, but in its *minor* form. It is
granted to children who cannot attain adult seriousness. If
the adult gives a major sense to childishness, if he writes
with the feeling that he is touching a sovereign value, he
has no place in Communist society. In a world from which
bourgeois individualism is banished, the inexplicable,
puerile humour of the adult Kafka cannot be defended.
Communism is basically the complete negation, the
radical opposite of what Kafka stands for.

BUT KAFKA HIMSELF AGREES

There was nothing he could have asserted, or in the name
of which he could have spoken. What he was, which was
nothing, only existed to the extent in which effective
activity condemned him. He was nothing but the
refutation of effective activity. That was why he bowed low
before an authority who denied him, although his way of
bowing was far more violent than a shouted assertion. He
bowed, and as he bowed, he loved and died, opposing the
silence of love and death to that which could never make
him yield, because the *nothingness* which can never yield in
spite of love and death, is sovereignly what it is.[25]

NOTES

1. Kafka, *Tagebücher* 1910–1923, Fischer Verlag, 1951; Heinemann, 1948–9.
2. I can make no other reply to Josef Gabel who has questioned this theory of mine (in *Critique*, no. 78, November 1953). The Oklahoma circus is not enough for us to introduce a historical perspective into Kafka's works.
3. Franz Kafka, *Hochzeitsvorbereitungen auf dem Lande und andere Prosa aus dem Nachlass*, Fischer Verlag, 1953.
4. Michel Carrouges, *Franz Kafka*, Labergerie, 1949.
5. F. Kafka, *Hochzeitsvorbereitungen* . . .
6. Of Joseph K., the hero of *The Trial*, who was clearly the author's double.
7. Carrouges, op. cit.
8. F. Kafka, *Tagebücher*. My italics.
9. Carrouges, op. cit.
10. F. Kafka, *Hochzeitsvorbereitungen* . . .
11. *La Part du Feu*, Gallimard, 1949.
12. Carrouges, op. cit.
13. F. Kafka, *Tagebücher*.
14. F. Kafka, *Hochzeitsvorbereitungen* . . .
15. Ibid.
16. F. Kafka, *Tagebücher*.
17. Ibid.
18. Carrouges, op. cit.
19. Ibid.
20. Ibid.
21. Here I feel I should quote a passage intended for another book:

> We are wrong to pay so much attention to the transition of the being from one form to another. Our disease is to know others as though they were *exteriors*, although they are no less *interior* than ourselves. If we imagine death, the void that it leaves obsesses us

because of our concern for ourselves, although the world is composed of wholes. But unreal death, which leaves the feeling of a void, attracts us at the same time as it disturbs us, because this void is connected with the fullness of being.

Nothingness, or the void, or others, are all equally close to an impersonal fullness – which is unknowable.

22. Carrouges, op. cit.
23. Ibid.
24. Ibid.
25. See above.

GENET

GENET AND SARTRE'S STUDY

From his earliest youth, a foundling proved that he had evil instincts by robbing the poor peasants who had adopted him. When he was reprimanded, he merely continued, escaped from the children's reformatory where he had had to be sent, stole still more than before and, on top of it all, prostituted himself. He lived in misery, begging and stealing, sleeping with everybody, betraying his friends, but nothing could stop him: he had chosen this moment to devote himself to evil. He decided to behave as badly as possible on every occasion and, when he realised that the worst crime is not to do evil, but to manifest it, he wrote his apologies of evil in prison. They were banned by law. Precisely because of this he could quit squalor, misery, prison. His books were printed and read, a producer with the Légion d'honneur staged one of his plays which was an incitement to murder. The President of the Republic commuted the sentence he was to serve for his latest crimes precisely because he had boasted of having committed them in one of his books. And, when he was introduced to one of his latest victims, the latter said: 'Delighted to meet you, Monsieur Genet. Please continue your misdemeanours.'[1]

'You will think this story unlikely,' Sartre continues, 'yet this is what happened to Genet.'

Nothing is more likely to astonish us than the character and work of the author of *A Thief's Journal*. Jean-Paul Sartre has now written a long book on the subject and I must immediately say that few books are of greater interest. Everything contributes to making it a monument: its length and the author's intelligence; the novelty and interest of the subject matter; the aggression which palpitates in each page; and a precipitous quality accentuated by repetition. The book conveys a feeling of confused disaster and universal fraudulence, but at the same time it illuminates the situation of modern man who rebels against, and rejects, everything outside himself.

Sartre is certain of an intellectual supremacy which, in a time of decomposition and transition, has little significance even in our own eyes. By giving us *Saint Genet* he has at last written the book which expresses himself. His faults have never been more obvious: never has he harped on his ideas for so long or shown a greater resistance to those subtle delights which chance introduces into our life and which give off a furtive but cheering light. His decision to depict horror with complacency proves this. The repetition is, in part, the result of a step which leads us away from the beaten track. But I also feel that the rigidity which inhibits moments of ingenuous happiness is unjustified, though what is limited by ingenuousness is at the opposite extreme from *awakening*. In this sense, though I am sometimes surprised, even as I laugh, I do not shut myself off from the contagion of those bitter exigencies which prevent the mind from coming to rest. Finally, there is nothing I admire more in *Saint Genet* than a passion for 'nullity', for the negation of the most attractive values, which reaches a form of perfection owing to the continuous expression of abjection. Even when Jean Genet describes his pleasure,

the accounts of his defilement have something disconcerting about them. But what happens when a philosopher
does so? . . . We must, I feel – and this is at least partly true –
turn our backs on what is possible and open ourselves to the
impossible without pleasure.

I regard this interminable study not only as one of the
richest books of our time, but as Sartre's masterpiece: never
before has he written something so striking, something
which escapes so forcibly from the habitual conventions of
thought. Genet's books were an excellent point of
departure: they allowed him to use to the full a shock value
and a turbulence whose outcome is worthy of him.
Through the object of his study, he has been able to bring
out the most vital points. This had to be said because *Saint
Genet* is not presented as the important work of a
philosopher. Sartre spoke of it in such a way that we are
entitled to be mistaken. Genet, he tells us,[2] 'has allowed his
complete works to be published with a biographical and
critical preface, as in the editions of Pascal and Voltaire in
the *Collection des Grand Ecrivains Français*' . . . I will pass over
Sartre's intention of extolling a writer who, though bizarre
and talented, is far from being on a level with the greatest:
Genet may be the object of a craze, but, bereft of a halo
given him by literary snobbery, it is Genet the man who is
worthy of interest, rather than Genet the writer. I shall not
insist. In all events it would be unjustified to regard Sartre's
massive study as a mere preface. Even if it has not fulfilled a
further purpose, this work of literature is nevertheless the
freest, most adventurous investigation a philosopher has
ever made of the problem of Evil.

TOTAL DEVOTION TO EVIL

The investigation is based on, though it is not exclusively
restricted to, Jean Genet's experience. Jean Genet has

chosen to explore Evil as others have chosen to explore Good. The absurdity of such an experiment is immediately obvious. Sartre is aware of this: we explore Evil in as far as we think it Good, and, inevitably, the exploration is doomed to failure or ridicule. But this does not make it any the less interesting.

To start with it is the revolt of a man banished from society. Deserted by his mother, brought up by the *Assistance Publique*, Jean Genet had all the less chance of being integrated within a moral community since he was intelligent. He stole, and after his first visit to a reformatory, prison became his doom. But if the outcasts of a retributive society have no 'means of overthrowing the established order...., they can see no other order', and there is nothing they admire so much as 'the values, culture and customs of a privileged caste... Only, instead of wearing their brand of infamy ashamedly, they flaunt it proudly.' 'Filthy nigger,' said a black poet. 'Well, yes! I am a filthy nigger and I prefer my blackness to the whiteness of your skin.'[3]

In this intial reaction Sartre sees the 'ethical stage of the revolt':[4] it is confined to 'dignity'. But the *dignity* in question is at the opposite pole to common dignity; the dignity of Jean Genet is the assertion of Evil. So he could never say, with Sartre's outraged simplicity, 'our abject society'. For him society is not *abject*. We can qualify it as such if we allow a justifiable contempt to pass before a care for precision. I can always call the most elegant man 'a bag of excrement', and, were it not powerless, society would reject what it found abject. For Genet it is not so much society that is abject, as himself: he would define abjection as *what he is*, as what he is passively – if not proudly. Besides, the abjection with which society is loaded is a small thing since it is the product of superficially corrupt individuals whose actions always have a 'positive content'. If these men had arrived at the same ends by honest means, they would have preferred them. Genet wants abjection even if it only brings suffering. He wants it for its own sake, beyond the commodities he finds in it. He wants it because of a vertiginous propensity towards an abjection in which he loses himself as completely as the ecstatic mystic loses himself in God.

SOVEREIGNTY AND THE SAINTLINESS OF EVIL

The association may be unexpected but it imposes itself to such an extent that Sartre, after quoting a phrase of Jean Genet, exclaims:[5] 'Surely these are not the laments of a mystic in moments of aridity?' This corresponds to Genet's fundamental aspiration towards sanctity, a word of which he says, mingling the taste for scandal with the taste for holiness, that it is 'the finest in the French language'. It accounts for Sartre's title, *'Saint' Genet*. The commitment to supreme Evil is indeed connected with the commitment to supreme Good, both being linked to each other by the stringency to which the other aspires. We cannot be mistaken about this stringency: never did the dignity or *sanctity* of Jean Genet have any other sense: abjection is the only path to them.

This sanctity is the sanctity of a clown painted like a woman who delights in being the object of derision. Genet represented himself as wearing a wig and prostituting himself, surrounded by figures who resemble him, and decked with a baroness's tiara of false pearls. When the tiara falls and the pearls spill he takes a set of false teeth out of his mouth, places them on his head, and exclaims, his lips sagging: 'Well, ladies! I shall be queen all the same!'[6] The fact is that aspiration to a horrible sanctity is allied to the taste for a *supreme decision*. This exasperated desire of

Evil appears by revealing the profound significance of holiness which is never greater than when it is reversed. There is an element of giddiness, an ascesis in this horror which Genet himself has tried to explain: 'Culafroy and Divine, with their delicate tastes, will always be forced to love what they abhor, and this constitutes a little of their sanctity because it is renunciation.'[7] The desire for sovereignty, to be sovereign, to love that which is sovereign, to touch it and impregnate oneself with it, fascinates Genet.

This elementary desire for sovereignty has varied and deceptive aspects. Sartre gives a grandiose side of it, going to the opposite extreme to Genet, whose shame, being the opposite of shame, is nevertheless shame. Sartre says:

> The experience of Evil is a princely *cogito* which reveals the singularity of consciousness before Being. I want to be a monster, a hurricane, all that is human is alien to me. I transgress all the laws established by man, I trample every value under foot, nothing of what *is* can define or limit me: yet I exist, I shall be the icy breath which will annihilate all life.[8]

Does that sound hollow? No doubt! But it cannot be separated from the stronger and dirtier flavour which Genet gives it: 'I was sixteen... there was no place in my heart where I could lodge the feeling of my innocence. I admit to being the coward, traitor, thief, queen which I was held to be... And I experienced the amazement of knowing that I was composed of filth. I became abject.'[9] Sartre has seen and understood this royal quality inherent in Jean Genet. If, he says, 'he so frequently compares prison to a palace, it is because he sees himself as a pensive and redoubted monarch, separated from his subjects, like so many archaic sovereigns, by unsurmountable walls, by taboos, by the ambivalence of holiness.'[10] The imprecision, negligence, and irony of this association correspond to Sartre's indifference to the problem of sovereignty.'[11] Yet Genet, who commits himself to the negation of every value, is no less committed to the enchantment of the supreme value, of what is holy, sovereign and divine. He may not be sincere in the pure sense of the word: indeed, he is never, can never, be sincere. But his obsession with sovereignty emerges when he describes a Black Maria as being clothed in the 'charm of haughty misfortune', of 'royal misfortune', when he sees 'a wagon loaded with greatness, fleeing slowly, as it transported [him], between the ranks of a crowd bowing in homage.'[12] The inevitable irony – but Genet has *succumbed* to this irony more than he *wanted* it – cannot stop us seeing the tragic bond between punishment and sovereignty: Genet can only be sovereign in Evil: sovereignty itself may be Evil, and Evil is never surer of being Evil than when it is punished. But theft has little prestige next to murder, or prison next to the scaffold. The true royalty of crime is that of the executed murderer. Genet's imagination tries to magnify it in a way that might seem arbitrary, but if, in prison, he braves solitary confinement and exclaims: 'I live on horseback... I enter other people's lives as a Spanish grandee enters the cathedral of Seville',[13] his boast is fragile and highly significant. His sadness when death looms up on all sides, when the criminal has caused it and awaits it, lends a fullness to the sovereignty he imagines. It is still fraudulent, no doubt, but, beyond the basic element which lacks both charm and happiness, is the world of man which is surely not all the effect of our imagination, a fiction? Often a marvellous effect, still more often an agonising effect. Socially the subtle magnificence of Harcamone in his cell is less imposing than that of Louis XIV at Versailles, but it has the same foundations. The verbal tinsel which Genet rarely spares us is veiled with gravity if he evokes Harcamone, in the darkness of a cell, 'like an invisible Dalai Lama . . . '[14] We cannot avoid a feeling of unease when we read the following sentence, an allegory of the murderer's execution: 'He was more decked in black than a capital whose king has just been murdered.'[15]

Like the obsession with sanctity, this obsession with royal dignity is a recurrent theme in Genet's work. I shall give further examples. Of a prisoner at Mettray, Genet writes: 'He said a single word which divested him of his quality as a prisoner but draped him in magnificent tinsel. He was a king.'[16] Elsewhere[17] he speaks of 'the whistling lads on whose heads can be seen a royal crown, like a halo.' Of Mignon Les Petits-Pieds, who sells his friends, he writes:[18] 'The people he passes . . . though they don't know him . . . confer on this stranger a discontinuous and momentary form of sovereignty. All these fragments of sovereignty mean that, at the end of his days, he will have passed through life like a sovereign.' Stillitano, to whom another prisoner once said, as a flea appeared on his collar, 'I can see a beauty climbing you', is also a king, 'a common king'.[19] Finally, Métayer, another prisoner at Mettray, 'was royal because of the sovereign feeling he had for his person.'[20] When he was eighteen, ugly and covered with red abscesses, Métayer said 'to the most attentive spectators, and above all to me, that he was descended from the Kings of France.' Genet adds:

Nobody has studied the idea of sovereignty in children. Yet I must say that there is not a child who, having under his eyes a history of France by Lavisse, Bayet or any other, has not thought himself a dauphin or some prince of the blood. The legend of Louis XVII's escape from prison gave an added pretext to these dreams. Métayer must have experienced them.

Yet Métayer would have had little to do with the royalty of criminals had he not been accused, perhaps wrongly, of having denounced an escape plan. Genet says:

> True or false, an accusation of this kind was terrible. One was cruelly punished on a suspicion. One was executed. This royal prince was executed. Thirty boys, fiercer with him than the knitting women were with his ancestors, surrounded him, screaming. In one of those silent pauses, which are frequently found in tornadoes, he was heard to murmur: 'They did this to Christ'. He didn't cry, but he sat on that throne draped in such a sudden majesty that he may have heard God himself say: 'You will be king, but the crown on your head will be of burning iron. *I saw him.*[21] I loved him.'

Genet's passion, affected but true, unites, in the same light and the same lie, this royalty of comedy (or tragedy) with that of the Divine queen, crowned by false teeth. Even the police force is cloaked in sinister and sovereign dignity by Genet's warped mysticism – the police force, 'a demonic organisation, as sad as the funeral rites, funeral ornaments, as prestigious as royal glory.'[22]

THE PASSAGE TO TREACHERY AND SORDID EVIL

The key to these archaic attitudes (archaic, but only to the extent in which the past, which is apparently dead, is more alive than modern appearances would indicate, is to be found in the most perverted part of *The Thief's Journal* where the author talks of a love affair which he had with a police inspector. 'One day,' he writes,[23] 'he asked me to "give" him some of my chums. When I agreed to do this I knew I was making my love for him deeper, but it is none of your business to know more.' Sartre wanted to leave no doubts about this point: Genet loves treachery, he sees in it the best and the worst of himself. A conversation between Genet and Bernardini, his lover, reveals the basis of the problem. He wrote:

> Bernard knew my life and never reproached me. Once, however, he tried to justify being a cop, and spoke about morals. Simply from an aesthetic point of view, I could not listen to him. The good will of moralists clashes with what they call my ill-faith.[24] If they can prove that an act is detestable because of the evil it causes, I alone can judge its beauty and elegance from the lyricism it arouses in me. I alone can refuse or accept it. I will never be led back to the right path. At the most, my artistic reeducation might be undertaken, though my educator would run the risk of being convinced by, and won over to, my cause – if its beauty were to be decided by the more *sovereign*[25] of the two personalities.

Genet has no hesitation about which authority to bow before. He knows that he is sovereign. This sovereignty of his cannot be sought: it is revealed, like divine grace. Genet recognises it by the lyricism it inspires. The beauty which inspires lyricism is an infraction of the law – of that which is forbidden and which is also the essence of sovereignty. Sovereignty is the power to rise, indifferent to death, above the laws which ensure the maintenance of life. It only differs from sanctity in appearance, the saint being the man whom death attracts, while the king is the man who attracts it to himself. Besides, we should never forget that the word 'saint' implies 'holiness', and that holiness is something forbidden, which is violent and dangerous, mere contact with which presages destruction: it is Evil. Genet is aware that he had an inverted image of sanctity, but he knows it to be truer than the other. This is the realm in which opposites are destroyed and conjoined. Only these abysses, these conjunctions, can give us the truth. The sanctity in Genet is most profound – it is the sanctity which introduces Evil, 'holiness', the earthly taboo. An inner sovereign need leaves him at the mercy of all that reveals a divine force beyond law. In something resembling a state of grace, he thus comes upon the arduous paths, to which his 'heart and his sanctity' lead him. 'The paths of sanctity,' he says, 'are straight, that is to say that we cannot avoid them, and when, by some misfortune, we have taken them, we cannot return. One becomes a saint by force of circumstance, which is the force of God!'[26] Genet's 'morals' are connected with a feeling of the heat, of the sacred contact given him by Evil. He lives enchanted, fascinated by the ensuing ruination. In his eyes nothing could compensate for this sovereignty and this sanctity, radiating from himself and others. The principle of classical morality is connected with the *survival* of being: that of sovereignty (or of sanctity) with the being whose beauty is composed of indifference to survival, of attraction, we might almost say, to death.

It is difficult to catch Genet out in this paradoxical position. He loves death, he loves punishment and ruination. He loves those sovereign guttersnipes to whom he gives himself, and he loves their cowardice. 'Armand's face was false, cunning, surly, evil, brutal... He was a brute. He laughed little and perfidiously... In himself, in his sexual organs which I imagined to be elemental, but of solid tissues and beautiful variegated shades, in his hot and generous bowels, I thought that he elaborated his desire to impose, apply and demonstrate hypocrisy, stupidity, wickedness, cruelty and servility and to abstract from them the most obscene domination over his whole person.' This detestable figure may have fascinated Genet more than any other. 'Gradually,' he writes, 'Armand became the

Almighty of morality.'[27] Robert tells Genet, who prostituted himself to old men and robbed them: 'Call that work? You attack old men who can only stand up thanks to their false collars and sticks.' But Armand's reply had to contain 'one of the boldest moral revolutions'. 'What do you think?' says Armand. 'When there's some use in it, *I* don't go for old men but for old women. Not for men but for women. And I choose the weakest. What I need is the money. A good job is a successful one. When you've realised that one doesn't work chivalrously, you'll have understood a lot.'[28] Once he had Armand's support, 'the code of honour among guttersnipes... seemed ridiculous' to Genet. One day he was to apply this 'will liberated from morality by Armand's reflection and attitude' to his way of 'considering the police': he was to plunge into sanctity and sovereignty. There would be no abjection, short of treachery, which would grant him this vertiginous and agonised majesty.

There is therefore an ambivalence: in his way Armand is sovereign; the beauty of his attitude proves its value. But Armand's beauty resides in contempt for beauty, in the preference for utility. His sovereignty is profound servility: a rigorous submission to self-interest. This runs counter to Harcamone's, less paradoxical, divinity. In Harcamone's case, crimes are never committed for motives of self-interest – the only reason for the second one, the murder of a prison warder, seems to be the delight in punishment. But Armand's attitude has a quality which Harcamone's murders lack: it is unforgivable, nothing redeems its shamefulness. Armand himself would refute any attribution of value to his acts apart from that of the basest motive, money: that is why Genet confers on his person incomparable value and true sovereignty. This presupposes two characters – or at least two opposite points of view. Genet demands the very deepest Evil, a radical opposition to

Good – that perfect Evil which is perfect beauty. He finds Harcamone relatively disappointing: in the end Armand is more alien to human feeling, more sordid and more beautiful. Armand is nothing but a precise calculator; he is no coward, but he resorts to cowardice because it pays. Is Armand's cowardice a hidden form of aesthetics? Does he have a disinterested preference for cowardice? He would then be at fault before himself. Genet, who sees into him, is the only one able to envisage his cowardice from an aesthetic point of view: he goes into raptures before him, as one might before a magnificent work of art. Armand won Genet's admiration by dismissing the possibility of admiration: even Genet would lose face before him if he admitted his aestheticism.

THE IMPASSE OF UNLIMITED TRANSGRESSION

Sartre has emphasised the fact that, by searching relentlessly for Evil, Genet has run into an *impasse*. In this *impasse* he seems to have found the least tenable position with regard to Armand's fascination, but it is obvious that what he really wanted was the impossible. This dominant sovereignty which one of the least sovereign of his lovers had for Genet entailed the greatest misery. Sartre has rightly pointed this out. 'The wicked man must want Evil for Evil's sake and . . . it is in the horror of Evil that he must find the attraction of sin.' Such is the radical notion of Evil which, according to Sartre, has been fabricated by 'honest men'. But, if the wicked man 'is not fascinated by Evil, if he does it out of passion, then . . . Evil becomes Good. In point of fact, he who loves blood and rape, like the butcher of Hanover, is a criminal lunatic, but he is not really wicked.'

I personally doubt whether blood would have had the same taste for the butcher if it had not been the blood of a crime, forbidden by the basic taboo with which law-abiding humanity opposes the lawless animal. I admit that, in Genet's case, his misdemeanours were freely asserted 'against his sensibility', solely to attract Sin. But it is not easy to decide about this point, any more than about certain other ones. Nevertheless, Sartre does so. Genet has experienced the climax of the forbidden, a delight that is familiar and elemental and yet closed to modern thought. That is why he has to 'draw his reasons (for doing evil) from the horror that (evil deeds inspired) him with and from his basic love of Good.' This is not as absurd as Sartre thinks: it is not necessary to stop at this abstract representation. I can take any example - the taboo against nudity which regulates social life today. Even if one of us pays no attention to this form of decency, his partner's nudity will excite his sexual impulses. From then on Good, which is decency, is his reason for doing Evil: an initial violation of the rule incites him, by contagion, to violate the rule still more. This taboo which we observe - passively, at least - only presents a slight obstacle in the way of a minor Evil, constituted by undressing one's partner. From then on Good, which is decency, is - and the author of *Being and Nothingness* finds this absurd - our very reason for doing Evil.

This example cannot be considered an exception. It seems to me that on the whole the question of Good and Evil revolves around one main theme - what Sade called irregularity. Sade realised that irregularity was the basis of sexual excitement. The law (the rule) is a good one, it is Good itself (Good, the means by which the being ensures its existence), but a value, Evil, depends on the possibility of breaking the rule. Infraction is frightening - like death: and yet it is attractive, as though the being only wanted to survive out of weakness, as though exuberance inspired that contempt for death which is necessary once the rule has been broken. These principles are bound up with human life. They are at the basis of Evil, of heroism or of sanctity. But Sartre does not acknowledge this[29]. They fail before Genet's excess. They presuppose a degree (a hypocrisy) which Genet rejects. The attraction of irregularity sustains the attraction of the rule. But, in that Armand seduced him, Genet deprived himself of both: self-interest alone remained.

Sartre's arguments resume their relevance where this avidity for crime is concerned: Genet's will is no longer the furtive will of any man, of any 'sinner', satisfied with a minimum of irregularity. It requires a general negation of the taboo, a search for Evil relentlessly pursued till the moment when every barrier has been broken and we reach a state of complete collapse. From then on Genet finds himself in the inextricable difficulty which Sartre has indicated: he lacks a motive to act. The attraction of sin is the essence of his excitement, but what if he denies the legitimacy of the taboo, what if the sin fails him? If it fails him, 'the Wicked man betrays Evil' and 'Evil betrays the Wicked man': a potentially unlimited desire for nothingness is reduced to vain agitation. What is vile is glorified, but Evil becomes pointless. That which wanted to be Evil is no more than a form of Good, and since its appeal was dependent on its power to destroy, it disappears in fulfilled destruction. Wickedness wanted to 'turn as much of being as possible into Nothingness. But since its action is realisation, Nothingness is transposed into Being and the sovereignty of the wicked man turns into slavery.'[30] In other words Evil becomes a duty, just as Good does. An unlimited weakness becomes evident; it affect disinterested crime and the basest calculation, open cynicism and treason. No taboo gives Genet the sensation of a taboo any more and, with numb senses, he finally founders. Nothing would remain unless he lied, unless a literary artifice enabled him to validate something, whose fraudulence he was aware of, for others. In the horror of no longer being tricked he moves towards his last resort - he tries to trick someone else in order to trick himself for an instant.

IMPOSSIBLE COMMUNICATION

Sartre himself noted a curious difficulty at the basis of Genet's work. Genet, the writer , has neither the power to communicate with his readers nor the intention of doing so. His work almost denies the reader. Sartre saw, though he drew no conclusions, that in these conditions the work was incomplete. It was a replacement, half way from the *major* communication at which literature aims. Literature is communication: a sovereign author addresses sovereign humanity, beyond the servitude of the isolated reader. If this is the case, the author denies himself. He denies his own peculiarities in favour of the work, at the same time as he denies the peculiarity of the reader in favour of reading. *Literary* communication - which is such in so far as it is poetic - is this *sovereign process* which allows *communication* to exist, like a solidified instant, or a series of instants, detached both from the work and from the reading of the work. Sartre knows this; he seems, though I cannot think why, to credit only Mallarmé, who certainly expressed it clearly, with a universal supremacy of communication over beings who communicate: 'In Mallarmé,' says Sartre, 'reader and writer are cancelled out simultaneously: they extinguish each other mutually, until the Word alone remains.'[31]

Instead of saying 'in Mallarmé', I would say 'whenever literature really appears'. However this may be, even if an apparent absurdity results from this process, the author was there to suppress himself in his work, and he addressed the reader, who read in order to suppress himself - or, if we prefer, to render himself sovereign through the suppression of his isolated being. Sartre speaks somewhat arbitrarily of a form of sacred or poetic communication in which the spectator or the reader feels himself 'changed into the thing'.[32] If there is to be communication, the person to whom the process is addressed momentarily changes himself into communication (the change is neither complete nor lasting, but it does, strictly speaking, *take place*: otherwise there is no communication). In all events communication is the opposite of *the thing* which is defined by the isolation into which it can be relegated.

In fact there is no communication between Genet and the reader – and yet Sartre assumes that his work is valid. He suggests that it is based on conversation, then on poetic creation. According to Sartre, Genet had himself 'consecrated by the reader'. 'To tell the truth,' he adds immediately, 'the reader has no knowledge of this consecration.'[33] This leads him to maintain that 'the poet ... demands to be recognised by an audience whom he does not recognise.' But this is unacceptable: I can assert that the consecrational operation, or poetry, is communication or nothing. Genet's work, whatever a commentator may say about it, is neither sacred nor poetic because the author refuses to communicate.

The idea of communication is difficult to understand in all its potentiality. I shall later try to convey a richness of which we are rarely conscious, but I would now like to insist on the fact that the idea of communication, which implies the duality rather than the plurality of those who communicate, appeals, within the limits of the communication in question, to their equality. Not only has Genet no intention of communicating when he writes, but, whatever his intention may be, in that a caricature or replacement of communication is established, the author refutes this fundamental analogy which the vigour of his work might reveal to the reader. 'His audience,' writes Sartre, 'bow before him, willing to acknowledge a liberty which they know full well does not acknowledge their own liberty.' Genet places himself if not above, at least outside, those who are called upon to read him. By putting out his hands, he forestalls any possible contempt, although his readers are rarely tempted to despise him: 'I acknowledge,' he says, 'that thieves, traitors, murderers, cheats have a profound beauty – a sunken beauty – which you lack.'[34]

Genet knows no rule of honesty: though he never actually says that he wants to laugh at his reader, this is what he does. This does not bother me, but I can just perceive that vague area where Genet's qualities are squandered. Part of Sartre's mistake is to take him literally. Only rarely – in the case of certain heart-rending themes – can we rely on what he says. Even then we must recall his indifference, his readiness to abuse us. In him, we arrive at that complete infringement of the laws of honesty which not even the Dadaists could achieve. For the Dadaists were honest in that they wanted nothing to have so much as a meaning. They wanted any proposition that appeared coherent to lose this deceptive appearance. Genet mentions 'an adolescent honest enough to remember that Mettray was a paradise.'[35] There is obviously something pathetic in the use of the word *honest* in this context: the reformatory of Mettray was a hell. To the severity of the warders was added the brutality of the prisoners. Genet himself has the 'honesty' to show that the children's gaol was the place where he discovered that infernal pleasure which made it a paradise for him. Yet the Mettray reformatory was not very different from the prison of Fontevrault (where Genet again met the 'adolescent' from Mettray). In most respects the population of the two gaols was the same. Now Genet, who frequently exalted prisons and their inmates, ended by writing:[36]

'Stripped of its sacred ornaments, I see the prison naked, and its nakedness is pitiless. The prisoners are mere wretches, their teeth rotting with scurvy, bent by illness, spitting, hawking and coughing. They go from the dormitory to the workroom in huge, heavy, noisy clogs, they drag themselves about on cloth slippers full of holes and stiff with dust and sweat. They stink. They cringe before the warders who are just as cowardly as they. They are nothing but an outrageous caricature of the handsome animals whom I saw when I was twenty, and I will never be able to reveal how hideous they have become sufficiently to avenge the harm they have done me, the boredom their unparalleled stupidity has caused me.

The point is not whether Genet's testimony is accurate, but whether he has written a work of literature, in the sense in which literature is poetry and profoundly, not just formally, sacred. I think I must insist, therefore, on the shapelessness of the aims of an author who is sustained solely by an uncertain instinct – a dissociated, tumultuous, but basically indifferent instinct, unable to reach the intensity of passion imposed by true honesty.

Genet himself never doubts his weakness. To create a work of literature can only be, I believe, a sovereign process. This is true in the sense in which the work requires its author to go beyond the wretch within himself who is not on the level of these sovereign moments. In other words the author must look, through and in his work, for that which denies his own limitations and weaknesses, and is not part of his profound *servitude*. He can then deny, safely and reciprocally, those readers without whose thought his work could not even have existed. He can deny them to the extent in which he has denied himself. That means that the idea of these indecisive beings, burdened with servility whom *he knows*, can make him despair of the work he has written. But each time these real beings bring him back to the humanity which never tires of being human, which never succumbs, and which always triumphs over the *means* of which it is the *end*. To produce a work of literature is to turn one's back on servility as on every conceivable form of diminution. It is to talk the sovereign tongue which, coming from that sovereign part of man, is addressed to sovereign humanity. Obscurely (often in an almost oblique manner, hindered by pretensions), the lover of literature feels this truth. Genet himself senses it, and he says:[37] 'The idea of a work of literature would make me shrug my shoulders.'

Genet's attitude is poles apart from any ingenuous representation of literature which may be considered pedantic but which, despite its inaccessible quality, is universally valid. Not that we should stop when we read 'I wrote to earn money.' Genet's work as a writer is worthy of attention. Genet himself is eager to be sovereign. But he has not seen that sovereignty involves the heart, it requires loyalty and, above all, communication. Genet's life is a failure and, though it has every appearance of success, so is his work. It is not servile; it is infinitely superior to most writings which are considered 'literary'; but it is not sovereign. It does not satisfy the elementary requirements of sovereignty – that ultimate loyalty without which the edifice of sovereignty would collapse. Genet's work is the fretting of a crotchety individual of whom Sartre said:[38] 'If he is pushed too far he will burst out laughing, he will immediately admit that he is laughing at our expense, that he has only tried to shock us further by calling that demoniacal and sophisticated perversion of a sacred notion "sanctity" ... '

Genet's indifference to communication means that his tales are interesting, but not *enthralling*. There is nothing colder, less moving, under the glittering parade of words, than the famous passage in which Genet recounts Harcamone's death.[39] It has the beauty of a piece of jewellery: it is too rich and in somewhat cold bad taste. Its splendour is reminiscent of Aragon's feats in the early days of surrealism – the same verbal facility, the same recourse to devices which shock. I do not believe that this type of provocation will ever lose its powers of seduction, but the effect of seduction is subordinated to the interest in a purely external success, to preference for a deception which can be immediately appreciated. The servility of the quest for this type of success is the same in the author and the reader. Each one, author and reader, avoids the pangs, the annihilation of sovereign communication. They both limit themselves to the prestige of success.

This is not the only aspect. It would be pointless to reduce Genet to what he managed to extract from his brilliant gifts. He has a basic desire for insubordination, but this desire, however profound, has not always corresponded to his work as a writer.

The most remarkable thing is that the moral solitude – and irony – into which he sinks have kept him outside that lost sovereignty, the desire for which brought him into the paradoxical situation I have mentioned. Indeed, the quest for sovereignty by the man alienated by civilisation is a fundamental cause of historical agitation (whether it be religious or political, undertaken, according to Marx, because of man's 'alienation'.) Sovereignty, on the other hand, is the object which eludes us all, which nobody has seized and which nobody can seize for this reason: we cannot possess it, like an object, but we are doomed to seek it. A certain utility always alienates the proposed sovereignty – even the celestial sovereigns, whom imagination should have freed from all servitude, subordinate themselves to useful ends. In *The Phenomenology of Mind*, Hegel pursues the dialectic of the *master* (the law, the sovereign) and the *slave* (the man enslaved by work) which is at the basis of the Communist theory of the class struggle. The slave triumphs, but his apparent sovereignty is nothing but the autonomous will for slavery: sovereignty must inhabit the realm of failure.

So we cannot talk of Jean Genet's failed sovereignty as if such a thing as the accomplished form of a real sovereignty existed. The sovereignty to which man constantly aspires has never even been accessible and we have no reason to think it ever will be. All we can hope for is a momentary grace which allows us to reach for this sovereignty, although the kind of rational effort we make to survive will get us nowhere. Never can we *be* sovereign. But we distinguish between the moments when fortune lets us glimpse the furtive lights of communication and those moments of disgrace when the mere thought of sovereignty commits us to seizing for it like a positive benefit. Genet's attitude, eager for royal dignity, nobility and sovereignty in the traditional sense of the word, is the sign of a calculation doomed to failure.

Let us take those many individuals who still study genealogy. Genet has a capricious and pathetic advantage over them. But the scholar who imposes titles on people demonstrates the same stupidity as Genet, who wrote these lines about the time when he travelled through Spain.[40]

Neither the guards nor the local policemen arrested me. The figure they saw was no longer a man, but the curious product of misery to whom laws cannot be applied. I had exceeded the limits of indency. No-one would have been surprised had I entertained a prince of the blood, a Spanish grandee, had I called him my cousin and talked to him in the finest words.

Entertain a Spanish grandee. But in what palace?

If I use this rhetorical procedure in order to show you the extent of the solitude which conferred sovereignty on me, it is because a situation, a success to be expressed by the words which should express the triumph of the century, impose it on me. A verbal relationship translates the relationship of my glory in terms of military glory. I was related to princes and kings by a sort of secret relationship, ignored by the world – that relationship which allows a shepherdess to be familiar with a king of France. The palace I talk of (for it has no other name) is the architectural combination of the increasingly tenuous refinements which pride imposed on my solitude.

If this passage is added to those already quoted it not only confirms Genet's predominant preoccupation with acceding to the sovereign part of humanity: it also emphasises the humble and calculating nature of this preoccupation, subordinated to a sovereignty whose appearance formerly constituted a historical reality. It emphasises the distance between the pretender characterised by his poverty, and the superficial successes of the royalty and aristocracy.

UNPRODUCTIVE CONSUMPTION AND FEUDAL SOCIETY

Sartre is aware of Genet's weakness – of his inability to communicate. He represents Genet as condemned to wanting to be a *being*, an unattainable object for himself, similar to things, not to consciousness – which is a subject, but a subject which cannot regard itself as a thing without ruining itself. (From beginning to end of his study, he never ceases to insist on this point.) In his eyes Genet is connected with a feudal society which imposes itself despite its outdated values. But this last weakness, far from making Sartre doubt the writer's authenticity, provides him with a means of defending him. He does not say, literally, that feudal society alone, the society of the past, based on landed property – and war – is guilty, but he seems to justify Genet on account of this archaic society which needed him, his crimes and his misery, in order to satisfy a tendency to waste and squander – to fulfil that end which is the destruction of goods, consumption. Genet's only moral wrong is to be the creature of a society which is not dead, but condemned – which is only in the process of disappearing. In all events, it is the wrong done by the ageing society to the new one, which is endeavouring to win the day politically. Sartre develops the contradiction between the reprehensible society, which is the 'consumer society' and the praiseworthy society, the 'productive society' which the Soviet Union strives to establish. Although these ideas are close to one that I myself expressed in *La Part Maudite. La Consumation* (Editions de Minuit, 1949), there is a basic difference. I emphasised the necessity of waste and the absurdity of productivity as an end. Yet I must say that Sartre is not consistent in his judgment of the consumer society. A hundred and fifty pages later, he twice uses the term 'society of ants' to designate that same 'productive society' to which he had previously referred as an ideal. Sartre's thought is more fluid than it sometimes seems.

One might as well say that Good and Evil are connected with the useful and the harmful. Of course certain forms of consumption are more useful than harmful, but these have little to do with pure consumption. They are forms of productive consumption which are at the opposite extreme of the feudal spirit of consumption for its own sake which Sartre condemns. He quotes Marc Bloch's[41] description of 'a curious competition of waste which once took place at a great "court" held in Limousin. One knight had a plot of land sewn with silver pieces; another burnt church candles in his kitchen; a third, "out of boastfulness", ordered all his horses to be burned alive.'[42] Sartre's reaction is obvious. It is that habitual indignation directed against all forms of consumption which are not justified by utility. He does not understand that useless consumption is as opposed to production as the sovereign is to the subordinate, and liberty to servitude. He will unhesitatingly condemn all that stems from a sovereignty of which I myself have acknowledged the 'basically' reprehensible nature. But what about liberty?

LIBERTY AND EVIL

To reveal Evil in liberty goes totally against a conventional and widespread way of thought. To start with, Sartre will deny that liberty must necessarily be Evil. But he endows 'productive society' with a worth, before acknowledging its relative nature: yet this worth is relative to consumption. It is essentially relative to unproductive consumption, that is to say, to destruction. If we seek the coherence of these representations, it soon transpires that liberty, even after the potential relationship with Good has been taken into account, is, as Blake said of Milton, 'of the Devil's party without knowing it'. Submission and obedience, on the other hand, are on the side of Good. Liberty is always open to revolt, while Good is as closed as a rule. Sartre himself talks of Evil in terms of liberty: 'nothing of what *is*,' he says[43] with reference to the 'experience of Evil', 'can define or limit me: yet I exist, I shall be the icy breath which will annihilate all life. So I will be *above* the essence: I do what I like, I do what I like to myself. . .' In all events nobody can proceed, as Sartre would apparently like to proceed, from liberty to the traditional concept of Good corresponding to utility.[44]

Only one path leads from the rejection of servitude to the free limitations of sovereign humour: this path, which Sartre does not mention, is the path of *communication*. It is only if *liberty*, the *transgression of laws* and *sovereign consumption* are envisaged in their true form that the foundations of a moral code are revealed for those people who are not entirely regulated by necessity and who do not want to renounce the fullness which they have glimpsed.

AUTHENTIC COMMUNICATION, THE IMPENETRABILITY OF ALL 'THAT IS', AND SOVEREIGNTY

The interesting aspect of Jean Genet's work does not reside in its poetic power, but in the lesson we can learn from its weaknesses. Similarly, Sartre's study is based less on a perfect understanding than on a determination to search for the areas of darkness.

There is a cold and fragile quality in Genet's writing which does not necessarily prevent us from admiring it, but which makes us hesitate to agree with him. Genet himself would reject agreement if, by some indefensible error, we wanted to agree with him. Since this communication fades away just when literature needs it, it leaves the impression of a grimace. It matters little if the mere sensation that there is something lacking reminds us of authentic communication. In the depression resulting from these inadequate exchanges, where a glassy barrier is maintained between the reader and the author, I am sure about one thing: humanity is not composed of isolated beings but of communication between them. Never are we revealed, even to ourselves, other than in a network of communications with others. We bathe in communication, we are reduced to this incessant communication whose absence we feel, even in the depths of solitude, like the suggestion of multiple possibilities, like the expectation of the moment when it will solve itself in a cry heard by others. In ourselves human existence is nothing but shouts, a cruel spasm, a giggling fit where agreement is born from a consciousness which is at last shared between the impenetrability of ourselves and that of others.[45]

Communication, in my sense of the word, is never stronger than when communication, in the weak sense, the sense of profane language or, as Sartre says, of prose which makes us and the others appear penetrable, fails and becomes the equivalent of darkness. There are various ways in which we talk in order to convince people to agree with us.[46] We want to establish humble truths which coordinate our attitudes and activity with those of our fellow human beings. This incessant effort to situate ourselves in the world with clarity and distinction would be apparently impossible if we were not first bound to one another by the feeling of *common subjectivity*, impenetrable in itself, and for which the world of distinct objects is impenetrable.

It is essential to understand the distinction between two sorts of communication, but this is difficult: they intermingle in that the emphasis is not on powerful communication. Even Sartre is a little confused about this. He saw, as he insists in *La Nausée*, the impenetrable nature of objects: in no wise do objects communicate with us. But he has not precisely defined the difference between object and subject. Subjectivity is clear in his eyes: it is that which is clear. On the one hand he seems inclined to minimise the importance of this intelligibility of the objects which we perceive according to the purpose we attribute to them; on the other, he does not pay enough attention to those moments of a subjectivity *which is always given us in the consciousness of other subjectivities*, to those moments when subjectivity seems unintelligible in relation to the intelligibility of customary objects and, more generally, of the objective world. He cannot overlook this appearance, but he turns away from the moments when we too are nauseated by it because, in the instant when intelligibility appears to us, it adopts an unsurmountable and scandalous quality in its turn. Finally, what *is*, for us, is scandal. Consciousness of being is the scandal of consciousness, and we cannot – indeed, we must not – be surprised.

But we must not be taken in by words. Scandal is the same thing as consciousness: a consciousness without scandal is alienated consciousness – a consciousness, experience proves it, of clear and distinct objects, intelligible, or thought to be so. The passage from intelligibility to unintelligibility, from that which, no longer being knowable, suddenly no longer seems tolerable to us, is certainly at the origin of this feeling of scandal, but it is less a question of difference of level than of an experience 'given' in the major communication of beings. The scandal is the *instantaneous* fact that consciousness is consciousness of another consciousness, that is the look of another look. In this way it is an intimate glow, removed from that which usually attaches consciousness to the lasting and peaceful intelligibility of objects.

If this is clear, we see that there is a fundamental distinction between *feeble communication*, the basis of profane society (of active society – in the sense in which activity merges with productivity) and *powerful communication* which abandons the consciousnesses that reflect each other, to that impenetrability which they 'ultimately' are. At the same time we can see that powerful communication is primary, it is a simple 'given', the supreme appearance of existence, which reveals itself to us in the multiplicity of consciousnesses and in their communicability. The habitual activity of beings – what we call 'our occupation' – separates them from the privileged moments of powerful communication which is based on the emotions of sensuality, festivity, drama, love, separation and death. These moments are by no means equal among themselves: we often look for them for themselves, but they only have a significance in the instant at which they appear, and it is contradictory to plan their repetition. We cannot obtain them by our own feeble means. But this does not matter: we cannot do without the reappearance, however agonising, of the instant when their impenetrability reveals itself to the consciousnesses which unite and penetrate each other unlimitedly. It is better to cheat than to be lacerated too cruelly or too definitively. With the scandal which we want to cause at all costs, but from which we also want to escape, we maintain an indefectible, but as painless as possible, a bond, in the form of religion or art (art which has inherited a part of the powers of religion). Literary expression always raises the problem of *communication*, and is indeed poetry or nothing – nothing but the quest for particular agreements or the teaching of those minor truths to which Sartre refers when he talks of prose.[47]

SOVEREIGNTY BETRAYED

There is no difference between this powerful communication and what I call sovereignty. *In the instant* in which it occurs communication presupposes the sovereignty of the individuals communicating with each other, just as sovereignty presupposes communication: either it is deliberately communicable, or it is not sovereign. We must insist that sovereignty is always communication, and that communication, in the powerful sense, is always sovereign. If we bide by this point of view, Genet's experience is of exemplary interest.

In order to convey the sense of this experience, which is not only that of a writer but that of a man who has broken every law of society – every taboo on which society is based – I should start with the human aspect of sovereignty and communication. In as far as it differs from animality, humanity is based on the observance of taboos, some of which are universal: the prohibition of incest, of contact with menstrual blood, of obscenity, murder and the consumption of human flesh; in the first place the dead are the objects of taboos which vary according to time and place, but which nobody should infringe.

Communication or sovereignty are 'given' whenever life is determined by certain general interdicts, as well as by countless local taboos. These different limitations infringe to various extents the fullness of sovereignty, so we must not be surprised if the quest for sovereignty is connected with the infringement of one or more interdicts. In Egypt, for example, the sovereign was exempt from the prohibition of incest. Similarly, the sovereign operation, sacrifice, has a criminal quality: to put the victim to death is to break a law which is valid in other circumstances. On a more general level behaviour contrary to profane laws is allowed, and sometimes even ordained, during those sovereign periods of festivity. The creation of a sovereign (or sacred) element, therefore, of an institutional figure or of a sacrificial victim, depends on the negation of some interdict, the general observation of which makes us human beings, as opposed to animals. This means that sovereignty, in that humanity tends towards it, requires us to situate ourselves 'above the essence' which constitutes it. It also means that major communication can only take place on one condition – that we resort to Evil, that is to say to violation of the law.[48]

Genet has a classical attitude in that he searches for sovereignty in Evil and that Evil does indeed provide him with those ecstatic moments when our very being seems to fall apart and, though it survives, escapes from the essence which limits it. But Genet refuses to communicate. By so doing he never reaches the sovereign moment, the moment when he would at last cease bringing everything back to his own obsession with isolation, or, as Sartre says, simply with 'being'. It is to the extent in which he abandons himself *completely* to Evil that communication escapes him. Everything becomes clear at this point. What holds Genet down is the solitude into which he shuts himself and where whatever subsists of other people is always vague and indifferent. He does the Evil to which he resorted in order to exist sovereignty for his own *benefit* alone. The Evil required by sovereignty is necessarily limited. Sovereignty itself limits it. It sets itself in opposition to all that enslaves it in as far as it is communication. It opposes itself with that sovereign instinct which expresses a sacred aspect of morality.

I admit that Genet wanted to become *sacred*. I admit that, in him, the *taste* for Evil went beyond personal interest, that he wanted Evil for a spiritual value, and that he lived his experience without flinching. No vulgar motive would account for his failure, but, as in a dungeon guarded more closely than real prisons, a ghastly destiny enclosed him within himself, at the depths of his mistrust. He never yielded completely to the irrational impulses which unite beings, but which unite them on the condition that they shed the suspicions and diffidence bred in the difference between each being. Sartre has given us a good account of this sullen sadness with which Genet is contorted.

A somewhat exaggerated literary admiration has not prevented Sartre from passing judgment on Genet. Indeed, it has enabled him to do so, and this judgment is of an astringent severity, tempered by a profound sympathy. Sartre insists on this point: although Genet, tormented by the contradictions of his desire for the worst, seeks 'the impossible Nullity',[49] he finally demands *being* for his existence. He wants to *seize* his existence. He must arrive at the *being*, he wants the *being* of *things* for himself... 'This existence' would have 'to be without risking its being: it would have to be *in itself*'.[50] Genet wants to 'petrify himself'. And, if it is true, as Sartre says it is, that Genet is searching for the point which Breton defined, in one of the best approaches to sovereignty, as the point 'where life and death, the real and the imaginary, past and future, the communicable and the incommunicable, the high and the low are no longer perceived in contradiction to one another... ', there must be a fundamental alteration. Indeed, Sartre adds: 'Breton hopes, if not to "see" the surreal, at least to merge with it in an indistinction where vision and being are all one...' But 'Genet's sanctity' is 'Breton's surreal understood as the inaccessible and substantial reverse of existence...'[51] It is sovereignty *confiscated*, the dead sovereignty of him whose solitary desire for sovereignty is the betrayal of sovereignty.

NOTES

1. Jean-Paul Sartre, *Saint Genet, comédien et martyr*, Gallimard, 1952; W. H. Allen, 1963 (*Oeuvres complètes de Jean Genet*). Sartre introduces his brief biography with the words: 'Here is a tale for an anthology of black humour.'
2. Sartre, ibid.
3. Sartre, ibid.
4. Ibid.
5. Ibid.
6. In *Notre-Dame des Fleurs, Oeuvres complètes*, t.II. Sartre analyses this coronation scene at length.
7. Ibid.
8. Sartre, op. cit.
9. quoted Ibid.
10. Ibid.
11. Sovereignty annoys him less than sanctity, whose stink reminds him of excrement. He sees its ambivalence, but he locates it in the disgust which he feels, 'whatever people may say', for fecal matter. He even talks of sovereignty in incontestable terms. 'If the criminal,' he says, 'has a strong head, he will want to remain evil until the end. That means that he will construct a system to justify violence, but at the same time this system will lose its sovereignty.' But he is not concerned with the problem of sovereignty, which every man has to solve on his own account, and which confronts man in general.
12. *Miracle de la Rose, Oeuvres complètes*.
13. Ibid.
14. Veiled with gravity, but it is still tinsel. Here is complete passage:

    > It is at the depths of this cell, where I imagined him like an invisible Dalai Lama, powerful and present, that he emitted his order of sadness, mixed with joy, throughout the prison building. He was an actor who

bore on his shoulders the burden of such a master-piece that one could hear him creak. Fibres were torn. My ecstasy was accompanied by a slight trembling, a sort of wave frequency, which was, alternatively and simultaneously, both my fear and imagination. Ibid.

15. Ibid.
16. Ibid.
17. *Notre-Dame des Fleurs, Oeuvres complètes, II.*
18. Ibid.
19. *Journal du voleur.*
20. *Miracle de la Rose.*
21. Genet's italics.
22. *Journal du voleur.*
23. Ibid.
24. Genet may here be alluding to his conversation with his friend Sartre.
25. My italics.
26. *Miracle de la Rose.*
27. *Journal du voleur.*
28. Ibid.
29. I remember a conversation after a lecture, when Sartre reproached me for my use of the word 'sin': I was not religious, and, in his eyes, my use of the word was incomprehensible.
30. Sartre, *Saint Genet.*
31. Ibid.
32. Ibid. At this point Sartre gives an excellent definition of the sacred: 'subjectivity manifesting itself in and through the objective by destroying objectivity'. Indeed, communication, whose supreme manifestation is reached through the consecrational process, necessarily bears on things, but things which are both denied and destroyed by it as such: sacred things are subjective. Sartre's error is to lapse into dialectical representations without a dialectical system, so that he constantly finds himself blocking the dialectical flux which he has set into motion. He is none the less profound, but he is disappointing. Would it be possible to confront so shifting a reality as the sacred, if we bound it

to that slow movement which contains both our own lives and historical life? By improvising, Sartre has lost the benefits of speed. He dazzles us, but all that remains is a truth which has to be questioned and digested *slowly*. His views are always significant, but they do no more than point to the right path.

33. Ibid.
34. *Journal du voleur.*
35. *Miracle de la Rose.*
36. Ibid.
37. *Journal du voleur.*
38. Sartre, *Saint Genet.*
39. At the end of *Miracle de la Rose.*
40. *Journal du voleur.*
41. *La Societé féodale*, quoted in *Saint Genet.*
42. In *La Part Maudite* Sartre might have found other examples of an instinct which, as I have proved, is universal.
43. *Saint Genet.* The italics are Sartre's.
44. The greatest difficulty encountered by Sartre in his philosophical studies is connected with his inability to pass from a moral of liberty to a common morality which binds individuals to each other in a system of obligations. Only a morality of communication – and loyalty based on communication – goes beyond utilitarian morality. But for Sartre, communication is not a basis; if he sees its possibilities it is through the opacity which beings present to each other. For him, it is the isolated being that is fundamental, not the multiplicity of beings in *communication*. So we await from him a work on morals which was announced after the war. Only the honest *Saint Genet* can give us an idea of what is in store for us. But *Saint Genet*, however rich, is by no means conclusive.
45. Where, we should add, sharing is possible, I must here pass over the deeper aspect of communication which depends on the paradoxical significance of tears. And yet I should observe that tears undoubtedly represent the height of communicative emotion and communication, but that Genet's coldness is at the opposite pole to this extreme emotion.

46. See *Saint Genet*.

47. Ibid.

48. I have frequently dwelt on the essential theme of law and transgression. The theory of transgression is primarily due to Marcel Mauss whose essays dominate modern sociology. Marcel Mauss, unwilling to formulate his ideas too definitely, has merely expressed them periodically in his lecture courses. But the theory of transgression has been the object of a brilliant study by one of his pupils. See Roger Caillois, *L'Homme et le Sacré*, enlarged edition with three appendices on sex, games, and war in their relationship to the sacred, published by Gallimard in 1950. Unfortunately Caillois' work has not yet attained the authority which it deserves, especially abroad. In this book I have shown that the distinction between law and transgression has dominated modern society no less than it dominated primitive society. It will soon appear that, whenever it is based on the interdict which opposes it to animal life, human life, at all times and in every form, is doomed, outside the domain of work, to the transgression which determines the transition from animal to man. (See my article in *Critique*, 1956, no. 111/112, August–Septem -ber 1956).

49. The term is Genet's and is quoted by Sartre (*Saint Genet*). In my opinion the quest for the 'impossible Nullity' is the form which the quest for sovereignty took in Genet's case.

50. Sartre, op. cit. The italics are Sartre's.

51. Ibid. My italics.